FLEXIBLE LEARNING

An Outline

GW00702363

Philip Waterhouse

Network Educational Press

Network Educational Press
Network House
Rode
Bath
BA3 6QA

First published 1990
© Copyright Network Educational Press

ISBN 1 85539 003 5

All rights reserved; no part of this publication may be reproduced, stored in a retrieval system, or transmitted in any form or by any other means, electronic, mechanical, photocopying, recording, or otherwise without the prior written permission of the Publishers. This book may not be lent, resold, hired out or otherwise disposed of by way of trade in any form of binding or cover other than that in which it is published, without the prior consent of the Publishers.

Bound in Great Britain by Redwood Press Ltd, Pegasus Way, Bowerhill, Melksham, Wiltshire.

Acknowledgements

Network Educational Press would like to thank all those publishers and the author, J B Thomas of Loughborough University, who allowed us to quote from their books. Extracts from HMI and National Curriculum documents are reproduced with kind permission of HMSO.

Contents

INTRODUCTION

The purpose of this handbook is to suggest approaches to the question
'What is Flexible Learning?' It does not aim to provide definitive
answers, but rather to provide the headings, with pointers for thought or
investigation. It is only an **outline**, an agenda for discussion about
flexible learning. It should be useful for those who, in their school or
college, are planning developments towards more flexible learning. It
can serve them as a **checklist** for matters to be considered. As such it
does not claim to discuss all the topics exhaustively; it is simply a
starter for discussion. Nor does it deal with the operational details;
these are tackled separately in other handbooks in the series.

There is nothing new in the idea of being flexible in one's approaches to
teaching and learning. Good teachers have always thought that way.
They have wanted to provide learning experiences which are sensibly
adapted to the needs of individuals, and they have sought to make whole
institutions into caring communities. They have been determined that
young people should be able to develop all their capabilities, personal as
well as intellectual.

So why have they found it so difficult? The answer lies partly in
tradition and partly in the nature of some of our institutions. The
following problems will be familiar enough:

- size of teaching groups
- length of lessons
- need for supervision
- demands of the examination system
- shortage of resources
- the belief of the person in the street that education is simply a
  matter of 'telling them'!

These problems are familiar enough and there is no need to elaborate.
Teachers are quite justified when they argue that the conditions under
which they work are not very supportive of the idea of **flexibility**. They
are working under a lot of pressure.

So why does it now seem that today's teachers in today's schools stand a
better chance of really making a difference to the ways in which
students learn and grow?

It is in three respects that things seem different today:

1) There is growing support for the *ideas* of flexibility from leading thinkers in education, psychology, sociology and management.

2) There is growing support for the *practice* of flexibility from government initiatives in the curriculum and in assessment.

TVEI, the GCSE, Scotland's **Standard Grade** and **CPVE** have been particularly influential in this respect. In 1989 the Training Agency has given formal recognition to the movement by establishing a *Flexible Learning Development Programme* within TVEI which is designed to help implement the underlying philosophy of TVEI. Details of the components of this programme are given in Appendix 1. Finally it will be argued in this handbook that the national curriculum is likely to become a powerful force for greater flexibility.

3) In the last two decades the profession has gained considerable experience in *implementing* flexible learning.

The **resource-based learning** movement in secondary schools and the **open learning** movement in further and higher education have been influential. Much of the experience has come through making mistakes, and this is encouraging because today's teachers are avoiding the clumsiness which characterised some of the earlier work in the sixties and early seventies.

So the ideas are there, the stimulus and encouragement of government is there, and the teachers are competent enough to rise to the challenge. But let us be under no illusion. It is a big challenge. It is to be hoped that if the profession can make the difference for the students, there will be differences too for the teachers themselves. Teachers need to be freed from the 'lock-step' of daily life in the schools. They will serve themselves and their students better when they broaden the repertoire of their activities and give themselves more discretionary time than they have at present.

The Outline of Flexible Learning

THE OUTLINE OF FLEXIBLE LEARNING

This outline offers a framework for thinking about flexible learning. It
will be useful when policies and long-term plans are being formulated.
It will serve as a checklist or an agenda, helping in the identification of
areas for development, and providing an integrated view of all the
teaching and learning within an institution.

The sources of inspiration and pressure

*A collection of quotes from authoritative sources which support the
ideas of flexible learning.*

- □ HMI
- □ The Psychologists
- □ The Futurologists
- □ The Managers
- □ The Poet/Philosophers
- □ The Researchers
- □ The National Curriculum
- □ GCSE
- □ TVEI

The goals of flexible learning

*An outline of the basic ideas which justify the shift towards more flexible
ways of organising teaching and learning.*

- □ The needs of society
- □ The needs of the individual

The contexts for flexible learning

*How the environment of education might be made more flexible to
enhance the quality of teaching and learning.*

- □ National pressures
- □ Institutional responses

Flexible learning and the curriculum

The changes that are taking place in the organisation of the school curriculum - the implications for flexible learning.

- ☐ The national curriculum
- ☐ 16 -19
- ☐ Institutional responses

Flexible learning and teaching methods

The styles, approaches, techniques and skills which support flexible learning.

- ☐ Counselling and guidance
- ☐ Individual action plans
- ☐ Study skills training
- ☐ Active learning approaches
- ☐ Tutorial support
- ☐ Use of library
- ☐ Management of private study
- ☐ Use of technology

Flexible learning and assessment

How flexible learning supports and is supported by new approaches to the assessment of students' learning.

- ☐ Profiling
- ☐ Profiles and records of achievement
- ☐ Continuous assessment
- ☐ Accreditation

Flexible learning systems

Whole systems of flexible learning, each of which has its own main emphasis and has thereby made its distinctive contribution to thinking and action within the whole field of flexible learning.

- ☐ Supported self-study
- ☐ Resource-based learning
- ☐ Open access workshops

- □   Open learning (institution based)
- □   Distance learning

The remainder of the handbook offers a short discussion under each of the headings of the outline.

Sources of Inspiration
and Pressure

SOURCES OF INSPIRATION AND PRESSURE

We should recognise that the thinking and inspiration of flexible learning come from a wide variety of sources. While it is true that the government initiatives in recent years have played a large part in stimulating action, the ideas themselves are not new. They are of ancient origin, and have been more strongly advocated during the present century by members of the teaching and related professions. The quotations come from all over the world; they belong to different eras; yet they all speak a common language!

A   ## HMI

The inspectorate has unrivalled access to evidence about the work of our schools. Two major reports have, in the last decade, been based on the inspection of schools: *'Aspects of Secondary Education'* (HMSO. 1979), and *'Secondary Schools: An Appraisal by HMI'* (HMSO. 1988).

The quotes on this page are entirely from the 1988 report. The major finding was that *"....three-quarters of the schools inspected were performing satisfactorily in general..."* But our quotes are concerned with the HMI anxieties about styles of teaching and learning.

Many lessons indicated that for the majority of pupils learning and teaching in terms both of pace, content and approach, have changed little since 1979. Pupils continued to spend a large part of their time in classrooms listening or writing; in the later years of school the total volume of their written work was usually considerable. Lessons often contained little to help pupils to apply what they had learned beyond the classroom. Successive lessons frequently followed a similar sequence of activities, and this contributed a sense of sameness and predictability to the pattern of the day. The requirements of external examinations and the need to 'cover the syllabus' were frequently advanced by teachers in explanation of the teaching methods which were adopted.

However, in more than half the lessons seen in sixth forms students spent a considerable proportion of their time as passive recipients of information; little opportunity was provided for discussion or the interchange of ideas and they undertook little independent reading and lacked appropriate study strategies.

B   THE PSYCHOLOGISTS

Psychologists have played a leading role in shaping thinking about education. It is the 'Humanistic' school that has had most influence on the thinking about teaching and learning styles. The first quote is a neat summary of the position of these academics; the second is from a well known passionate advocate of more flexible learning approaches.

The basic principle of learning in perceptual-humanistic psychology has been stated as follows: Any information will affect a person's behaviour only in the degree to which he has discovered the personal meaning of the information for him. This means that learning is a subjective matter, having to do with what goes on in the personal experience of the student. Effective teaching in such a frame of reference is not a matter of managing behaviour and manipulating curricula; it is a matter of facilitation, of encouraging, and of ministering to processes going on within the student. This principle helps us to understand why so much teaching has little effect on the student. It also points directions in which we must explore to improve the system.

(Combs W. Fostering Maximum Development of the Individual .. in Issues in Secondary Education: Yearbook of NSSE. 1976. New York.)

It has a quality of personal involvement.
It is evaluated by the learner.
Its essence is meaning.

(Carl Rogers. Freedom to Learn. C E Merrill. Columbus, Ohio. 1979.)

C   ## THE FUTUROLOGISTS

Some exciting reading has come in recent years from the pens of those
who try to combine a deep and broad knowledge of present society with
a vision of possible futures.

Over the long pull, however, we can expect education also to
change. More learning will occur outside, rather than inside, the
classroom. Despite the pressure from unions, the years of
compulsory schooling will grow shorter, not longer. Instead of
rigid age segregation, young and old will mingle. Education will
become more interspersed and interwoven with work, and more
spread out over a lifetime. And work itself - whether production
for the market or prosumption for use in the home - will
probably begin earlier in life than it has in the last generation or
two. For such reasons, Third Wave civilisation may well favour
quite different traits among the young - less responsiveness to
peers, less consumption-orientation, and less hedonistic
self-involvement.
Whether this is so or not, one thing is certain. Growing up will
be different. And so will the resultant personalities.

(Alvin Toffler. The Third Wave. Pan. London. 1983.)

The correct policy would be to open as many diverse paths as
possible, with plenty of opportunity to backtrack and
change...Most of the money now spent for high schools and
colleges should be devoted to the support of apprenticeships,
travel, subsidised browsing in libraries and self-directed study
and research.... rural reconstruction, and work camps for projects
in conservation and urban renewal.

*(Paul Goodman. Freedom and Learning: the Need for Choice. Saturday Review. May
1968.)*

D THE MANAGERS

Some valuable insights into the processes of education come from the ranks of the industrial managers. While their products may be different to ours, most of their concerns are, like ours, with people.

Suppose however that more teachers taught people not subjects, or, rather, managed the learning of a group of pupils, their whole learning, not just their learning of one subject: the form teacher, in other words. Educationally this releases the teacher to be an educator in the full and rounded sense of that term. Organisationally it turns the pupil from a product into a group member, a co-worker, the kind of relationship that exists in most primary schools....A teacher's expertise in a subject probably becomes more important as the pupil becomes more advanced and learns more. But as pupils learn more they also grow up and become more responsible for managing their own learning, moving to the client model of the sixth form, where teachers are resources to pupil clients. Organisationally, either the primary school model of co-worker, with teacher/manager or the sixth-form model of clients and resources is more desirable than the factory model of the secondary school, because of the possible effect on the individual pupil. Do we really need anything to intercede between the co-worker and the client model.

(Charles Handy. Taken for Granted? Understanding Schools as Organisations. Longmans. London. 1984.)

Achieving flexibility by Empowering People:

1. Involve everyone in everything.

2. Use self-managing teams.

3. Listen, celebrate, recognise.

(Tom Peters. Thriving on Chaos. Pan. London. 1988.)

E   ## THE POET/PHILOSOPHERS

In moving language the Persian poet, Kahlil Gibran, captures the
sentiment of those teachers and parents who approach their role as
educators with a sense of great responsibility and humility. And the
ancient Chinese philosopher, Lao tsu, provides a neat affirmation.

Your children are not your children. They
are the sons and daughters of Life's longing
for itself.
They come through you but not from you.
And though they are with you yet they belong
not to you.
You may give them your love but not your
thoughts,
For they have their own thoughts.
You may house their bodies but not their
souls,
For their souls dwell in the house of tomorrow,
which you cannot visit, not even in your
dreams.

You may strive to be like them, but seek not
to make them like you,
For life goes not backward nor tarries with
yesterday.

You are the bows from which your children as
living arrows are sent forth.

Let your bending in the archer's hand be for
gladness.

(Kahlil Gibran)

When the best leader's work is done,
The people say,
'We did it ourselves'.

(Lao tsu)

F   ## THE RESEARCHERS

The following extract is from a survey of the literature of the
self-concept conducted by J B Thomas for the National Foundation for
Educational Research.

Self-concept research is saying to the teacher: you are the
backbone of the education system, not the social scientists or the
armies of advisers and petty officialdom. The teacher is a force
in the classroom and in the field of self-concept he is a force for
good given he has the will to experiment and succeed. Teachers
can enhance the self-concept through the provision of special
curriculum materials, through encouraging more personal and
private talks with pupils in calm, supportive atmospheres
avoiding domination, threatening and sarcastic situations,
through developing experimental curriculum projects designed
to enhance self-worth in children, and in general through
becoming more person orientated in the classroom.
We are at the beginning again. Asked to consider our
educational objectives. No one can deny that education is facing
a crisis from economic and other factors. There is little the
teacher can do as teacher to improve society outside the gates of
the school but a great deal that can be done to improve society
inside the school. Not all our children are academic, by ability
or inclination, but neither are all our pupils models of laziness
and vandalism. Many are in need of help, perhaps more than we
realise. Teachers are on the verge of a teaching revolution and
teachers and pupils alike face the same depersonalising threats of
modern technological society. Only by seeing teaching as one of
the helping professions and less an elitist procedure for
purveying knowledge can we encourage a positive sense of
worth not only in our pupils but in ourselves.

(J B Thomas. The Self in Education. NFER. Slough. 1980.)

G · THE NATIONAL CURRICULUM

Many teachers initially feared that the national curriculum would have
an undesirable effect on their freedom to adapt what they teach to the
needs of individual students. They were anxious to retain their right to
try out new approaches to teaching and learning, and to develop in their
students those aspects of personal development which may not fit too
easily into a syllabus or attainment target. However the consultation
document gave reassurance on these matters.

> The Secretaries of State believe it to be important that schools
> should also have flexibility about how they organise their
> teaching. The description of the national curriculum in terms of
> foundation subjects is not a description of how the school day
> should be organised and the curriculum delivered. The clear
> objectives for what pupils should be able to know, do and
> understand will be framed in subject terms. Schools will be able
> to organise their teaching in a variety of ways.

> There must be space to accommodate the enterprise of teachers,
> offering them sufficient flexibility in the choice of content to
> adapt what they teach to the needs of the individual pupil, to try
> out and develop new approaches, and to develop in pupils those
> personal qualities which cannot be written into a programme of
> study or attainment target.

(National Curriculum 5-16 Consultation Document, HMSO 1987)

H · GCSE

The influence of the GCSE has been widely recognised. From the point
of view of flexible learning there have been three significant
innovations.

1. The importance attached to course work. In most subjects the
student's final mark depends not simply on the result of the written
examinations, but also on the student's performance in regularly
assessed work throughout the two year course. In many subjects this is
as high as 20%.

2. The much stronger attachment to the principle of criteria-referenced
grading. In this grades are defined and awarded in terms of
predetermined standards of performance specific to the subject

concerned. Candidates are required to demonstrate predetermined levels of competence in specified aspects of the subject in order to be awarded a particular grade. The effect of this has been to emphasise what students know and can do. Eventually employers and colleges will have a much better idea of what candidates have achieved.

3. The single system of examinations, with a single scale of grades. The built-in flexibility is an improvement on the old system in which schools and students had to make early decisions about which examination to prepare for.

TVEI

The influence of TVEI on styles of teaching and learning has been profound. Here is the mission statement.

WHAT IS TVEI?

TVEI's role is to help produce a more highly skilled, competent, effective and enterprising workforce for the 1990s. It is a bold long term strategy, unique amongst nations for investing in the skills of ALL our young people 14 - 19 in full-time education and equipping them for the demands of working life in a rapidly changing highly technological society. It does this by:

- relating what is learnt in schools and colleges to the world of work;

- improving the skills and qualifications for all; in particular in science, technology, information technology and modern languages;

- providing young people with direct experience of the world of work through real work experience;

- enabling young people to learn to be effective, enterprising, and capable at work through active and practical learning methods;

- providing counselling, guidance, individual action plans, records of achievement and opportunities to progress to higher levels of achievement.

(TVEI Statement. January 1990.)

The **TVEI Flexible Learning Project** has stipulated this definition of flexible learning.

FLEXIBLE LEARNING: WHAT IS IT?

As the name implies, flexible learning is a means of delivering the curriculum involving the flexible use and management of a range of human resources, materials, activities and situations more accurately to meet the learning needs of students as individuals. This will allow learning to be optimised. Additionally, it will also encourage the learner to take responsibility for his/her own learning, with ownership devolved to the learner so that s/he can more easily apply the experience in a wide variety of situations including life-long learning.

(Training Agency. 1989.)

The Goals of Flexible Learning

The Needs of Society

The Needs of the Individual

THE GOALS OF FLEXIBLE LEARNING

The goals of flexible learning can be expressed in terms of the needs of society and the needs of the individual learner. This is a huge subject quite outside the scope of a small handbook. So the notes are simply intended as pointers to the main arguments which seem to support the ideas of more flexible learning.

A   **The Needs of Society**

The demands of working life

> .....equipping them for the demands of working life in a rapidly changing highly technological society.

The TVEI mission statement seems at first sight to be a hard imposition that is aimed solely at increasing the Gross National Product. Yet this can be argued differently. Human beings thrive on stimulus and challenge. There is a basic urge to produce or to provide services for others. This urge is social in its origin; work can be the source of great personal satisfaction, and most people seek meaningful activity and meaningful relationships at work. Of course, making this possible is the responsibility of management, but increasingly working people want to design their own working environment and to take on greater responsibility. Hence the emphasis in education programmes on **responsibility, initiative and enterprise.**

The ecological ethic

A strong emphasis within our current society is the recognition that human beings belong to and are part of the natural world. Hence our concern for 'Green' issues: we are worried about the scarcity of natural resources, and we have a strong sense of responsibility for the environment and for future generations. This emphasis is outward looking and at first sight it might seem to contradict the concern for individual experience and self-development which is so strong an influence in flexible learning. In fact, the two ethics are complementary. Together they encourage cooperation and a balanced *people in their natural environment* approach to all development.

The movement towards World unity

This sense of 'One World' exists both in a political sense and in an economic one. Of course the movement has a long way to go and there are powerful obstacles. Nevertheless it is a major social reality for our time and it is making heavy demands on the members of our society. The demands are mainly to do with maturity, at personal, community, national and international levels. This demands of all individuals greater self-awareness, the ability to take a detached view of one's own perceptions and loyalties, the capacity for imagination, and the power of empathy.

The speed of change

A major additional influence is the speed at which changes now take place in our society. Underlying it all is technology which increases both the volume and the speed of communication. For the citizen of the 21st century survival will surely depend on the ability to adapt, to learn new skills, to acquire new understanding, to seize opportunities, to take initiative, and to display enterprise.

B   The Needs of the Individual

Individual differences

A basic understanding which supports the move towards flexible learning is that of individual differences. There is a great danger of over-simplification; individual differences are multidimensional:

- **Cognitive** differences include 'general intelligence', language skills, specific aptitudes, developmental readiness, problem-solving ability, critical thinking, learning styles.
- **Personal** differences must take into account general attitude to school and learning, emotional stability, motivation.
- **Social** differences must take into account friends, family, neighbourhood, school.

One of the main arguments for flexible ways of organising learning is that the system stands a better chance of tuning in to individual differences and adapting the teaching and learning arrangements accordingly.

Autonomy

It has been argued that autonomy is a fundamental aim of education. The concept is certainly given high priority by those who are involved in flexible learning. An analysis of the concept will provide the justification for these beliefs.

The short definition of autonomy is that it is the power or right of self-government. In personal terms this is commonly extended to the idea that human beings carry within them their own guiding principles. Just how far this idea can be carried is open to debate. Teachers certainly do try in practice to foster some of the attributes of autonomy within their students. They are concerned to help them to be less dependent, and to be capable of making decisions for themselves.

But on the other hand they are conscious that inter-dependence is a social reality and is a valuable element in the lives of most of us. So it is not the blind and stupid pursuit of self-will that we are advocating; rather a balance that respects these three important connotations of the concept of autonomy.

- Autonomous judgements, thoughts and actions are made with a sense of **responsibility.** This implies considerably more than the mere exercise of self-will.

- Autonomous judgements, thoughts and actions are made in a **rational** way.

- Autonomous judgements, thoughts and actions are **authentic.** This has connotations of sincerity, credibility, consistency, of being genuine and true to oneself.

4

The Contexts for Flexible Learning

National Pressures

Institutional Responses

– Flexitime

– Flexispace

– Fleximoney

– Flexipeople

Education Otherwise

THE CONTEXTS FOR FLEXIBLE LEARNING

In the last analysis all management in education can be reduced to the management of time, the management of space, the management of money, and, last but certainly not least, the management of people. This section considers how the management of these variables can contribute to flexibility and so help in making progress towards the goals of flexible learning.

Getting more **time,** more **space,** more **money,** and more and better **people** are worthwhile ambitions for teachers and LEA officials. However it would be unwise to believe that nothing can be achieved in flexible learning until substantial improvements in these matters have been achieved. The fact is that a lot of splendid work in flexible learning has been achieved with the resources already available. It would be quite wrong to defer getting started in flexible learning on the grounds that it needs extra resources.

The truth of the matter is that flexible learning, like any other system for education, will benefit greatly from more resources. But the wise teacher will recognise that the small amount of extra resources tends to be attracted to the work that is already under way. And he or she will act accordingly!

The following sections set out some of the possibilities within each of these areas. In keeping with the aims of the handbook they do not pursue to the end; they are simply headings for an agenda or a checklist for decision and action.

A ## National Pressures

Increasingly decisions made at national level are bearing down on the work of institutions and individual teachers.

This is not the place to attempt a detailed analysis of all these pressures. But the diagram opposite identifies them, and shows that the environments in the institutions are changing in response to these pressures. A short discussion of these institutional responses follows on page 24.

NATIONAL PRESSURES

NATIONAL CURRICULUM

TVEI   •   GCSE

CHANGES FOR 16 – 19s

LMS

NEW VOCATIONAL
QUALIFICATIONS

INSTITUTIONAL RESPONSES

TEACHING AND LEARNING STYLES

B   ## Institutional Responses

FLEXITIME

Within the class period

The problems of the 35 minute period

In an attempt to respond to all the competing claims on the timetable many schools have been forced into organising in very short periods of time. Life is dominated by the school bell. The heavy demands of the National Curriculum could reinforce this state of affairs.

Very short teaching periods tend to produce lessons **without variety.** Allowing for the bits of *housekeeping* which have to be done on arrival and dismissal, there is time only for a short stint on the substance of the lesson. This situation forces the teacher to pack as much as possible into the time available, and the result is a **heavy reliance on whole class teaching.**

Schools which have addressed themselves to this problem usually argue that it is better to offer students fewer big blocks of time than the larger number of smaller blocks. Thus two one-hour periods (total 120 minutes) is preferred to four 35 minute periods (total 130 minutes).

The bigger block of time lends itself to, indeed demands, variety. Most teachers with these big blocks of time allocate part of the period to individual or small-group work. And *housekeeping* takes up a smaller percentage of the total time available.

The trend towards bigger blocks of time is marked, and has now asserted itself in subjects like mathematics and modern languages in which teachers in the past have argued the case for daily exposure in very short periods. If the trend can be sustained in face of the contrary influences it will prove to be a gain for all teachers who are committed to more flexible styles of working.

Variety within the class period

The lack of variety in classroom experience is one of the most common points made by those who have had the opportunity to observe classroom work in a systematic way. The short class period is an important factor in determining this. Even in these conditions however it should be possible to extend outwards beyond *chalk and talk*. The following checklist of activities indicates the main types that are available to the teacher. Each type of activity has an infinite number of variations on the theme:

- teacher exposition/presentation

- recitation - in which under the control of the teacher the students respond verbally to questions and instructions

- individual 'seat work' (an American expression!) in which the students work individually on a set assignment with the teacher carrying out a monitoring role

- small group work under the teacher direction, with the remaining students on 'seat work'

- small group work carried out independently of the teacher, but subject to the teacher's control through processes of briefing and review

- *housekeeping* activities - very necessary, but they must not be subject to Parkinson's Law (expanding the work to fill the time available! Research has shown that lessons can vary greatly according to the amount of time spent 'on task').

It is in the **balance** between whole class work, individual, paired and small group work that the flexibility is achieved. This is how the sense of sameness which HMI reported in their 1988 survey can be avoided. Young people, more than most, desperately need **protection from monotony.**

Organising a lesson with this kind of variety makes special demands on the teacher. Hence the current interest in 'classroom management'. **A separate handbook in the series is entirely devoted to this important subject.**

Within the school day and week

The pattern of the school day has tended to work against greater flexibility in learning. The day has been equally divided into periods, usually of short duration and the periods allocated to the subject departments. This state of affairs has been the direct result of pressure for better time allocations from the subject departments. Some early indications are that the National Curriculum demands could reinforce these.

It is to be hoped that this will not prove to be so, because school life could benefit so much from greater flexibility in the school day and week. Of course some flexibility already exists, particularly in the use of private study and of homework. Some brief pointers to the possible ways ahead now follow.

Private Study

Time for private study has always been available to sixth form students. Many schools are now extending the arrangement to younger students, particularly those in the fourth and fifth years with their heavy course work commitments for GCSE and Standard Grade.

Although private study in schools has been around for a long time results, on the whole, have been disappointing. Many teachers complain that their sixth form students seem incapable of the self-discipline and systematic organisation that private study demands. Some schools insist that private study is supervised, but, even that only partly solves the problem. So the prospects for extending private study down into the main school do not seem, at first, to be particularly promising.

The way ahead, for sixth formers and for younger students alike, is to tackle the problem at source. Some of the principles are listed below.

- All teachers responsible for students with private study time **must** accept a role in training their students in study skills and personal organisation.

- This implies being much more involved in decisions about the students' private study time. All the decisions about **what** to do, **when** to do it, **where** to do it, **how** to do it, should be regarded as negotiable between teacher and each individual student. It is quite wrong to leave students entirely on their own in this matter. Most of them need guidance.

- This in turn demands briefing in advance of new learning tasks and systematic review of the work that has been completed. It is only through **detailed discussion before and after a piece of work** that students acquire the skills and strategies of effective learning.

- **Private study needs to be started as early as possible.** It is unrealistic to provide no opportunities or experience in the lower school and then to expect instant achievement in the upper school.

- There is much to be said for the idea of using **non-specialist support** for students engaged on private study. This could involve the form tutor, for example, or a teacher who has particular interests in study skills or resources, or a librarian. Young people often value the help of a sympathetic adult who makes no claim to subject expertise, but who offers wisdom and experience of a more general nature in addition to and complementary to the support that the subject specialist can offer.

Many of the arguments about private study apply with equal force to homework. Homework should not be associated with **tedium and monotony;** the work that students do at home should be exciting and motivating. Teachers can get the best out of it and make it serve the goals of flexible learning by attending to some of the principles suggested below:

- The homework should have a **natural link** with the work that is being done in class.

- The great **variety** of possibilities should be recognised and exploited. As well as more conventional work involving reading and notetaking, there should be opportunities to practise skills to achieve mastery, and to relate the work being done to the world outside school by using resources that are available in the home or in the community (and that includes people).

- The small regular tasks traditionally associated with homework may be inadequate for the programmes of study now being followed by our senior pupils. Longer assignments may be more appropriate, but these need careful management by the teacher: systematic **briefing**; regular **review;** and the **marshalling of resources** in support of the students.

Flexitime on the timetable

A timetable which has some built in flexibility has been produced by a number of schools. Most have achieved this by extending the operating time for the whole institution. This does not mean necessarily extending the working day for either teachers or students, but it does demand greater flexibility from them. For example, in some systems teachers and students may find that their work pattern varies from day to day - different starting and finishing times, different times for lunch break, and so on.

For many the flexible day still retains the conventional pattern for the morning and this covers a large part of the school curriculum. After lunch greater flexibility is achieved by giving students more choices over short periods of time; by offerings which are extra-curricular, not only in the traditional sense of clubs and sports, but also offering additional study opportunities. This last arrangement can result in a wide range of 'clinics', support classes, talent development, and experiential learning. The key points are the student choice and the short module pattern of organisation.

Some schools achieve flexibility through a more modest adjustment to the weekly timetable. Time is set aside on a regular weekly basis for the kinds of opportunities described in the previous paragraph. This has the virtue of being much simpler administratively.

Within the school year

The same kind of principles can also be applied to the school calendar. The idea of an alternative timetable, or even several alternative timetables, which operate for limited times during the school year, can be very productive. In the past this arrangement has been much used as a means of arranging visits and field work with the minimum disruption of the normal timetable; the idea being simply to concentrate all the disruption into as small a period as possible. Often the arrangements were on a grand scale, involving large numbers of students.

More recently the same principle has been used to challenge subject departments to make the kinds of provision which the teachers have argued could not be made because of timetable constraints. This has led to a rich variety of activities:

- counselling - especially in terms of academic progress
- specialist workshops
- talent development
- 'clinics'
- expeditions and visits of all kinds in small groups
- private study
- community work
- enterprise and work experience.

Some of the most interesting experiments on these lines have resulted from a very simple alternative timetable in which a whole year group has been allocated in big blocks of time to a single faculty. The challenge to the staff is an exciting one, and teachers often respond in most imaginative and flexible ways. In such a way the stock of experience in managing flexible learning grows rapidly.

FLEXISPACE

The unkindest view of our secondary schools is of big buildings divided into classrooms of about the same size, each containing about 30 students listening to the words of a teacher. Unfortunately many teachers do find themselves forced into that situation and are obliged to expend considerable effort in order to break free. The suggestions which follow can't possibly be made to work in all situations, but they are worth considering nevertheless.

Within the classroom and the subject department

A desirable starting point is the concept of the departmental suite, which might consist of a cluster of classrooms, rooms for administration, storage space, a resource base, and additional space for students working independently.

Not many departments are likely to enjoy such an environment, but it is useful to have a vision in mind so that opportunities can be seized whenever they present themselves.

Thinking can start with the individual classroom. Most are dreadfully cluttered. We do need space for storage, but most of our classrooms are too heavily dedicated to it. As a consequence our students are packed like sardines and the scope for flexible working is limited. Consider these possibilities:

- Aim to get all long term storage banished from the classroom in the interests of providing more working space for the students. If adequate store rooms do not exist then special arrangements need to be made: for example, the use of cloakroom areas and corridors (with high level wall units if regulations will not allow the use of floorspace).

- Arrange for classrooms to be functionally specialised (eg a room devoted exclusively to lower school teaching in the subject). This cuts down the amount of resource material that is kept in the room itself.

- Work to the principle that only resources in current use should be housed in the classroom.

- Consider arranging the students' furniture round the periphery of the room rather than in the middle. The middle is best occupied by resources. This arrangement is a more interesting use of space, and lends itself to greater flexibility.

- Enhance the work of the departments by providing a good resource centre.

- Aim to have an efficient system of storage and retrieval which is thoroughly explained to all users.

- Allow students direct access to the resources. This means they will have to be trained to be responsible users.

- Provide some seats and tables for users.

- Find space for the students who need to work independently. It is often best to provide individual carrels and to locate them close to the staff headquarters, or alternatively to disperse them throughout the departmental area. The great mistake would be to provide a large number close together which were totally unsupervised.

Within the school as a whole

The School Library

Thinking should start with the library. Most school libraries are far too small. Apply a simple test: can the library seat more than 10% of the school population in dignified individual work stations as well as providing adequate space for all the book stock and other media resources? Most school libraries will fail the test. Yet the 10% objective should be regarded as a **minimum** not an optimum.

What can be done obviously is a matter for local decision. Many schools faced with this situation have found it possible to extend the library by taking over adjacent space. This needs to be done with care and sensitivity: a private study area needs to have a library atmosphere and this means carpets; well-designed work stations; some comfortable chairs; a small selection of dictionaries, atlases, single volume encyclopedias. and other commonly used reference books; and facilities for using audio-visual media.

The 'Study Hall'

This was a common feature of American High Schools in the fifties and sixties. The basic idea is to provide a large number of work stations in one large area with constant supervision. This can then be used by any student with private study time or can be used by class teachers as a way of releasing small numbers of students to private study tasks with the assurance that they will be supervised.

Although the arrangement is not now so popular there is no reason why it cannot be made into a useful service. Some attention needs to be given to the lay out and general atmosphere (see notes above on private study in libraries), and also to the role of the supervisor, who would contribute to the success of the service by taking on a role of counsellor and non-specialist tutor. Some schools have found this kind of arrangement particularly valuable for fourth and fifth year students.

Studying everywhere

Ultimately almost the entire premises of the school should offer study facilities. Secondary teachers need to look at the best practice in our primary schools to see examples of this principle in action. In some of these schools it seems that every nook and cranny is furnished with a table and a few chairs, and the children are dispersed in twos and threes among them. So it is not only a question of encouraging the departments to find space but also to find space which could be available more generally.

Many schools are, quite rightly, concerned about the supervision implications of this, and it is wise to proceed cautiously, at first setting up a few such stations which are easily monitored. But undoubtedly the school which moves in this direction succeeds in creating a much more civilised environment.

Beyond the school boundaries

This idea is hardly new and schools have recognised the need for students to get their knowledge and experience as much as possible from the 'real' world out there. So a checklist is sufficient, simply to reveal the range of possibilities without exploring the detail of any of the ideas.

- Field work in a number of school subjects
- Work with the local community
- Work experience
- Use of public libraries
- Use of information services of public and private bodies
- Projects and surveys of various kinds
- Visits and expeditions
- Participation in events
- Taking part in competitions

FLEXIMONEY

The ways of managing the finances of schools are undergoing a major change with the introduction of LMS (local managment of schools). At this early stage most schools are still concerned with the rules and procedures under which the system will operate. It may be some years before schools are able to feel confident with the new system and to start exploiting its flexibility.

However there is every chance that the special needs of individuals and small minority groups may benefit from the fact that the school will be able to make local decisions about funding.

Local funding may also prove beneficial to those schools that wish to mount substantial development programmes in flexible learning. This will be so much better than sending one member of staff on a course. The whole school will be able to commit itself to a programme involving initial awareness raising, systematic training, opportunity for development, and thorough evaluation of what has has been achieved. A number of schools, using the greater freedom of devolved INSET budgets, have already demonstrated their ability to mount this kind of programme sharply focused on the needs of the school.

FLEXIPEOPLE

The secondary school has been traditionally staffed on the basis of subject specialism. Most teachers in the system describe themselves as subject specialists. They assume likewise that they are not competent to teach other subjects, and are reluctant to make even tiny excursions into territory that they regard as belonging to someone else.

This is unfortunate for the schools. Most teachers seriously underestimate their own **general** skills as educators. They have maturity, experience as learners themselves, competence in study skills and in personal organisation, a command of language, and experience in applying the tests of reason to all situations.

The implication of this is that teachers can and should offer their **general** skills to their students, not as a substitute for specialist support, but as an **essential complement** to it. It is a lucky student who has not only the support of a good specialist but also the **additional** support of a teacher who is not a specialist. The non-specialist has certain advantages: he/she is not so threatening as the specialist; he/she often is starting where the student is now and so becomes a **co-worker**; he/she is offering the student more **time** to engage in deliberation about the subject, and it is simply **time** that many students need to get to grips with their problems.

So teachers need to be encouraged to intervene more in the learning processes of the students for whom they have a responsibility.

- This means more scope being offered to the form tutor, beyond the 'pastoral' domain.

- It means encouraging teachers with library responsibilites to take every opportunity to regard themselves as supporting tutors, not merely as organisers of resources.

- It means enhancing the role of private study supervisor into that of *learning support teacher*, a move that has been made recently by a number of schools.

- It means building on the excellent work already being done by special needs teachers within the classrooms of the subject specialists. It is hard to find a subject specialist who is not grateful and full of praise for this kind of support.

Of course falling rolls in schools has had the effect of broadening the scope of many teachers as the demand for their particular speciality has fallen. Provided the extension has been made willingly and with determination it will have been beneficial not only to the school's organisation, but also to the students and the teachers involved.

Greater flexibility in the deployment of teachers must be to the advantage of the learners. Most teachers will benefit from a broadening of their contribution to the academic life of the school.

C Education Otherwise

Many parents have chosen to arrange their children's education themselves, finding the pressures and styles of institutional life uncongenial. The organisation which supports them is called 'Education Otherwise', a name derived from the wording of the 1944 Education Act ...

> It shall be the duty of the parent of every child of compulsory school age to cause him to receive efficient full-time education suitable to his age, ability, and aptitude, either by regular attendance at school or otherwise.

Although many teachers feel opposed to this kind of arrangment there has been a softening of attitude in recent years. The school is no longer thought of as having sole and exclusive rights in the matter of young people's education. It aims to develop a partnership with parents and with other members of the community. It recognises the importance of experiences and relationships created outside the boundaries of the school.

Considerable flexibility is already apparent in some institutions, both public and private, catering for the needs of the 16 - 19 year groups. These concentrate on careful tutorial support in preparation for A-level examinations while not demanding full-time attendance. The assumption is that students will make their own arrangments for the remainder of their time, either through part-time work or through registration with other educational organisations.

Of particular interest will be the development of the **'Open School'** which is now carrying out feasibility studies. The inspiration came from **Lord Michael Young** who has been involved in so many national initiatives leading to more flexible kinds of learning.

To extend this degree of flexibility into the main school area would certainly present the schools with additional work, but it could be argued that many students would benefit considerably. And it might prove to be a better solution for that increasing number of parents who are attempting to go it alone, and who experience considerable difficulties and only limited success.

NETWORK
EDUCATIONAL
PRESS

To the Head of English

English Literature
Activities and Assignments Guides

*A series of photocopiable guides which support
flexible styles of teaching and learning*

- **wide range of texts**
- **varied, imaginative learning methods**
- **differentiated assignments**
- **oral assessment assignments**

To be published November 1990

Editor: Chris Griffin
*Deputy Head, Pewsey Vale School, Wiltshire
Co-author of "English Matters"*

Design: Mike Cousins
*Deputy Head, The Ferrers School, Northamptonshire
Co-author of "English Matters"*

and

Dave Gill
Head of English, The Ferrers School, Northamptonshire

The Merchant of Venice	*William Shakespeare*
Macbeth	*William Shakespeare*
Romeo and Juliet	*William Shakespeare*
The Long, The Short and The Tall	*Willis Hall*
The Scarecrows	*Robert Westall*
Children of the Dust	*Louise Lawrence*
Z for Zachariah	*Robert O'Brien*
1984	*George Orwell*
Animal Farm	*George Orwell*
The Crucible	*Arthur Miller*
Of Mice and Men	*John Steinbeck*
It's My Life	*Robert Leeson*
Our Day Out	*Willy Russell*
A Breath of Fresh Air	*Geraldine Kaye*
Narrative of the Life of Frederick Douglass, an American Slave	*Frederick Douglass*
An Inspector Calls	*J B Priestley*

**NETWORK
EDUCATIONAL
PRESS**

The Teaching and Learning Series

*A series of practical handbooks on
teaching and learning styles*

· TEACHING AND LEARNING ·
· NEW SERIES ·

BOOK 1 Flexible Learning: An Outline by Philip Waterhouse

Philip Waterhouse presents an outline of all the key issues related to teaching and learning styles:

- *sources of inspiration and pressure*
- *the goals of flexible learning*
- *flexible forms of assessment*
- *flexible methods*
- *flexible learning and the curriculum*
- *the contexts for flexible learning*
- *systems of flexible learning*

The book is, in essence, a handbook, ideal for reference or as a catalyst to new thinking. It provides the perfect agenda for individual, team or whole staff planning and INSET.

Books 2 – 5 examine in more detail key areas outlined in Book 1.

BOOK 2 Classroom Management by Philip Waterhouse

The book looks at the classroom mechanics of teaching and learning:

- *preparing the classroom: space, furniture, fittings, equipment, layout*
- *whole class teaching: exposition, dialogue, active learning*
- *developing independent learning: progressive training, overcoming weaknesses, supervised study*
- *the small group tutorial, the self-managing team*
- *interpersonal relationships*
- *a framework for the improvement of classroom management.*

The book is full of advice both for the classroom teacher and for the department or curriculum manager looking for INSET strategies.

BOOK 3 Resources for Flexible Learning by Robert Powell

Robert Powell argues that flexible styles of teaching and learning can best be delivered by making more imaginative use of existing resources. He suggests several ways in which this can be done and provides practical advice on all aspects of resource management:

- *defining, choosing and evaluating resources*
- *using and preparing study guides*

**NETWORK
EDUCATIONAL
PRESS**

Study Guides
Writers' Workshops

Network Press is planning a series of 2 day practical workshops on the use and preparation of study guides.

The workshops will be held on a regional basis all over England and Wales. The courses will run by Rob Powell co-founder of Network Press, a former Deputy Head & TVEI Co-ordinator.

Day 1 – *The potential, use, design and presentation of study guides; the use of desk-top publishing*
Day 2 – *Preparing a study guide.*

✂ —

Please send me further details of courses in my region

Name ....

Position ....

Institution ....

Address ....

....

.... LEA/Borough ....

Telephone No. ....

**Send to – Network Educational Press
(Ref. Study Guide Course)
P O Box 635
Stafford ST18 0LJ**

- *adapting resources, assignment writing, differentiation, building student self-esteem*
- *design and layout of resources, the use of desk-top publishing*
- *integrating the use of the library/resource centre, enhancing the role of library/resource centre personnel*
- *planning a module to integrate teaching and learning styles, information skills, use of resources and cross-curricular themes*
- *whole school issues, INSET, use of teacher time*

The book will provide support to teachers, librarians and those seeking to adopt a whole school approach to the use of resources.

BOOK 4   Tutoring   by Philip Waterhouse

Philip Waterhouse explores the potential and techniques of small group tutoring:

- *the rationale and objectives of tutoring*
- *the contexts for tutoring*
- *arrangements for tutoring*
- *tutoring styles & techniques*
- *INSET strategies*

The book will be invaluable to all those seeking to improve the quality of guidance and support given to students.

BOOK 5   What Makes a Good School?   by Tim Brighouse

Tim Brighouse examines the many whole school issues which influence the quality of teaching and learning.

- *leadership in the successful school*
- *creating a successful environment*
- *supporting staff*
- *reviewing for successful planning and practices*
- *organising and maintaining success*

He seeks to answer the question so often posed by Headteachers, Governors, Teachers and Parents. His solutions, a mixture of sound theory, vision and pragmatism, will enlighten, stimulate and challenge all those with an interest in better schooling.
The inter-chapter cameos of the best and worst of school practice will provide much food for thought.

Order Form
Please photocopy the order form if you wish to keep this brochure

Name	Position

Institution

Address	
	LEA/Borough

Order No.	Signature

Please send me: Cost

	copies of Book 1 *Flexible Learning: An Outline*	
	copies of Book 2 *Classroom Management*	
	copies of Book 3 *Resources for Flexible Learning*	
	copies of Book 4 *Tutoring*	
	copies of Book 5 *What Makes a Good School?*	
	Total	

Each Book **£4.50** per copy
30 copies of any book, or combination of books, can be purchased at £4.10 per copy.
Further discounts for bulk orders negotiable.

PLEASE NOTE. The high cost of invoicing for small amounts means we are unable to invoice for orders of less than **£18.00** (4 books). **Cheques with order are required for orders of 3 books or less.**

If you would like more copies of this brochure to distribute to staff at INSET meetings please indicate number required below.

Please send me	*brochures*

All publications are available direct from the publishers:
Network Educational Press, PO Box 635, Stafford, ST18 0LJ
Telephone: 0889 271300

The guides provide a fresh and imaginative approach to English Literature and will appeal to:

- *experienced teachers looking for new ideas*
- *teachers new to particular texts*
- *student teachers*
- *non - specialists*

The guides are non-prescriptive and teachers of English will welcome a format which allows selective and flexible use of a range of suggested activities. Each guide has 3 sections:

- *a summary of key plot events (for easy reference)*
- *a collection of varied learning activities*
- *a collection of assignments*

The activities seek to develop a wide range of student skills:

- *oral skills*
- *paired and small group work*
- *improvisation and role play*
- *discursive, narrative and creative writing*

The assignments engage the student in a detailed study of the text, are clearly differentiated, and seek to provide:

- *a critical understanding of plot, character and style*
- *suggestions for the open study or extension work*
- *scope for independent research*
- *coursework opportunities in English*

The guides will be enormously helpful to students studying texts independently or revising for examinations.

Guide Authors:

Mike Cousins, Deputy Head, Ferrers School, Northamptonshire

Dave Gill, Head of English, Ferrers School, Northamptonshire

Rob Hill, Head of English, Highwood School, Nailsworth, Gloucestershire

John Hobbs, Head of English, Pewsey Vale School, Wiltshire

Nick Manns, Head of English, Queen Elizabeth School, Corby, Northamptonshire

Margaret Simmonds, Latham School, Skelmersdale, Lancashire

Tim Small, Deputy Head, Peers School, Littlemore, Oxfordshire

Andy Stables, Lecturer in Sec. English Education, University College, Swansea

Illustrator: Dave Cousins, Bradford College of Art and Design

Order Form

Please photocopy the order form if you wish to keep this brochure

Name	Position

Institution

Address	
	LEA/Borough

Order No.	Signature

Please send me:

[ ] copies of the English Literature activity/assignment pack

Each photocopiable pack **£24.00** (+£2.60 p+p)
Cheque with order price **£22.00** (+£2.60 p+p)

Cheques made payable to: Network Educational Press   Total [ ]

We regret that we are unable to sell individual titles within the pack.

Other titles available from Network Press: tick for details

Flexible Learning: An Outline	**Philip Waterhouse**	£4.50	[ ]
Classroom Management	**Philip Waterhouse**	£4.50	[ ]
Resources For Flexible Learning	**Robert Powell**	£4.50	[ ]
Tutoring	**Philip Waterhouse**	£4.50	[ ]
What Makes A Good School?	**Tim Brighouse**	£4.50	[ ]

Photocopiable Study/Enquiry Guides available now – 30 titles in each pack:
(tick for details)
Humanities ❐ Geography ❐ Business Studies ❐ £35.00 per pack
Available Spring term 1991: English Lanugage ❐ History ❐
Science ❐ Design and Technology ❐

All publications are available direct from the publishers:
Network Educational Press, PO Box 635, Stafford, ST18 0LJ
Telephone: 0889 271300

**NETWORK
EDUCATIONAL
PRESS**

The Teaching and Learning Series

*A series of practical handbooks on
teaching and learning styles*

BOOK 1   Flexible Learning: An Outline by Philip Waterhouse

Philip Waterhouse presents an outline of all the key issues related to teaching and learning styles:

- *sources of inspiration and pressure*
- *the goals of flexible learning*
- *flexible forms of assessment*
- *flexible methods*

- *flexible learning and the curriculum*
- *the contexts for flexible learning*
- *systems of flexible learning*

The book is, in essence, a handbook, ideal for reference or as a catalyst to new thinking. It provides the perfect agenda for individual, team or whole staff planning and INSET.

Books 2 – 5 examine in more detail key areas outlined in Book 1.

BOOK 2   Classroom Management   by Philip Waterhouse

The book looks at the classroom mechanics of teaching and learning:

- *preparing the classroom: space, furniture, fittings, equipment, layout*
- *whole class teaching: exposition, dialogue, active learning*
- *developing independent learning: progressive training, overcoming weaknesses, supervised study*
- *the small group tutorial, the self-managing team*
- *interpersonal relationships*
- *a framework for the improvement of classroom management.*

The book is full of advice both for the classroom teacher and for the department or curriculum manager looking for INSET strategies.

BOOK 3   Resources for Flexible Learning by Robert Powell

Robert Powell argues that flexible styles of teaching and learning can best be delivered by making more imaginative use of existing resources. He suggests several ways in which this can be done and provides practical advice on all aspects of resource management:

- *defining, choosing and evaluating resources*
- *using and preparing study guides*

- adapting resources, assignment writing, differentiation, building student self-esteem
- design and layout of resources, the use of desk-top publishing
- integrating the use of the library/resource centre, enhancing the role of library/resource centre personnel
- planning a module to integrate teaching and learning styles, information skills, use of resources and cross-curricular themes
- whole school issues, INSET, use of teacher time

The book will provide support to teachers, librarians and those seeking to adopt a whole school approach to the use of resources.

BOOK 4   Tutoring   by Philip Waterhouse

Philip Waterhouse explores the potential and techniques of small group tutoring:

- the rationale and objectives of tutoring
- the contexts for tutoring
- arrangements for tutoring
- tutoring styles & techniques
- INSET strategies

The book will be invaluable to all those seeking to improve the quality of guidance and support given to students.

BOOK 5   What Makes a Good School?   by Tim Brighouse

Tim Brighouse examines the many whole school issues which influence the quality of teaching and learning.

- leadership in the successful school
- creating a successful environment
- supporting staff
- reviewing for successful planning and practices
- organising and maintaining success

He seeks to answer the question so often posed by Headteachers, Governors, Teachers and Parents. His solutions, a mixture of sound theory, vision and pragmatism, will enlighten, stimulate and challenge all those with an interest in better schooling.
The inter-chapter cameos of the best and worst of school practice will provide much food for thought.

Order Form

Please photocopy the order form if you wish to keep this brochure

Name	Position

Institution

Address	
	LEA/Borough

Order No.	Signature

Please send me: Cost

	copies of Book 1 *Flexible Learning: An Outline*	
	copies of Book 2 *Classroom Management*	
	copies of Book 3 *Resources for Flexible Learning*	
	copies of Book 4 *Tutoring*	
	copies of Book 5 *What Makes a Good School?*	
	Total	

Each Book **£4.50** per copy
30 copies of any book, or combination of books, can be purchased at
£4.10 per copy.
Further discounts for bulk orders negotiable.

PLEASE NOTE. The high cost of invoicing for small amounts means we are
unable to invoice for orders of less than **£18.00** (4 books). **Cheques with order
are required for orders of 3 books or less.**

If you would like more copies of this brochure to distribute to staff at INSET
meetings please indicate number required below.

Please send me	*brochures*

All publications are available direct from the publishers:
**Network Educational Press, PO Box 635, Stafford, ST18 0LJ
Telephone: 0889 271300**

**NETWORK
EDUCATIONAL
PRESS**

To the Head
of English

English Literature
Activities and Assignments Guides

*A series of photocopiable guides which support
flexible styles of teaching and learning*

- ● **wide range of texts**
- ● **varied, imaginative learning methods**
- ● **differentiated assignments**
- ● **oral assessment assignments**

To be published November 1990

Editor: Chris Griffin
*Deputy Head, Pewsey Vale School, Wiltshire
Co-author of "English Matters"*

Design: Mike Cousins
*Deputy Head, The Ferrers School, Northamptonshire
Co-author of "English Matters"*

and

Dave Gill
Head of English, The Ferrers School, Northamptonshire

A wide range of literary texts

The Merchant of Venice	*William Shakespeare*
Macbeth	*William Shakespeare*
Romeo and Juliet	*William Shakespeare*
The Long, The Short and The Tall	*Willis Hall*
The Scarecrows	*Robert Westall*
Children of the Dust	*Louise Lawrence*
Z for Zachariah	*Robert O'Brien*
1984	*George Orwell*
Animal Farm	*George Orwell*
The Crucible	*Arthur Miller*
Of Mice and Men	*John Steinbeck*
It's My Life	*Robert Leeson*
Our Day Out	*Willy Russell*
A Breath of Fresh Air	*Geraldine Kaye*
Narrative of the Life of Frederick Douglass, an American Slave	*Frederick Douglass*
An Inspector Calls	*J B Priestley*

The guides provide a fresh and imaginative approach to English Literature and will appeal to:

- *experienced teachers looking for new ideas*
- *teachers new to particular texts*
- *student teachers*
- *non - specialists*

The guides are non-prescriptive and teachers of English will welcome a format which allows selective and flexible use of a range of suggested activities. Each guide has 3 sections:

- *a summary of key plot events (for easy reference)*
- *a collection of varied learning activities*
- *a collection of assignments*

The activities seek to develop a wide range of student skills:

- *oral skills*
- *paired and small group work*
- *improvisation and role play*
- *discursive, narrative and creative writing*

The assignments engage the student in a detailed study of the text, are clearly differentiated, and seek to provide:

- *a critical understanding of plot, character and style*
- *suggestions for the open study or extension work*
- *scope for independent research*
- *coursework opportunities in English*

The guides will be enormously helpful to students studying texts independently or revising for examinations.

Guide Authors:

Mike Cousins, Deputy Head, Ferrers School, Northamptonshire

Dave Gill, Head of English, Ferrers School, Northamptonshire

Rob Hill, Head of English, Highwood School, Nailsworth, Gloucestershire

John Hobbs, Head of English, Pewsey Vale School, Wiltshire

Nick Manns, Head of English, Queen Elizabeth School, Corby, Northamptonshire

Margaret Simmonds, Latham School, Skelmersdale, Lancashire

Tim Small, Deputy Head, Peers School, Littlemore, Oxfordshire

Andy Stables, Lecturer in Sec. English Education, University College, Swansea

Illustrator: Dave Cousins, Bradford College of Art and Design

Order Form
Please photocopy the order form if you wish to keep this brochure

Name	Position

Institution

Address	
	LEA/Borough

Order No.	Signature

Please send me:

[　　　] copies of the English Literature activity/assignment pack

Each photocopiable pack **£24.00** (+£2.60 p+p)
Cheque with order price **£22.00** (+£2.60 p+p)

Cheques made payable to: Network Educational Press　　Total [　　　]

We regret that we are unable to sell individual titles within the pack.

Other titles available from Network Press:　　　　　　　tick for details

Flexible Learning: An Outline	**Philip Waterhouse**	£4.50	
Classroom Management	**Philip Waterhouse**	£4.50	
Resources For Flexible Learning	**Robert Powell**	£4.50	
Tutoring	**Philip Waterhouse**	£4.50	
What Makes A Good School?	**Tim Brighouse**	£4.50	

Photocopiable Study/Enquiry Guides available now – 30 titles in each pack:
(tick for details)
Humanities ❐ Geography ❐ Business Studies ❐ £35.00 per pack
Available Spring term 1991: English Lanugage ❐ History ❐
Science ❐ Design and Technology ❐

All publications are available direct from the publishers:
Network Educational Press, PO Box 635, Stafford, ST18 0LJ
Telephone: 0889 271300

▲ Supported Self-Study

▲ Active Learning

▲ Links with the Community

▲ 90 different titles

An Introduction written by

PHILIP WATERHOUSE

provides advice on how these guides can be used for whole class, group or independent learning.

Reduced front page of Business Studies Unit 13:
Planning for Changes in the Workforce.

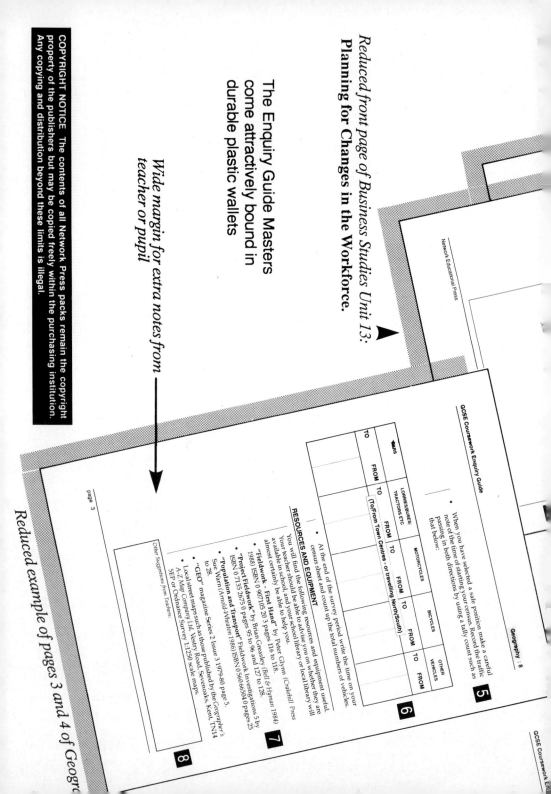

The Enquiry Guide Masters
come attractively bound in
durable plastic wallets

Wide margin for extra notes from
teacher or pupil

COPYRIGHT NOTICE The contents of all Network Press packs remain the copyright
property of the publishers but may be copied freely within the purchasing institution.
Any copying and distribution beyond these limits is illegal.

Network Educational Press

GCSE Coursework Enquiry Guide

Geography : 8

- When you have selected a safe position make a careful
  note of the time of starting your census. Record the traffic
  passing in both directions by using a tally count such as
  that below:

5

BUS	LORRIES/BUSES/ TRACTORS ETC	MOTORCYCLES	BICYCLES	OTHER VEHICLES
FROM TO	FROM TO	FROM TO	FROM TO	FROM
	(To/From Town Centres - or travelling North/South)			
TO				

6

- At the end of the survey period write the time on your
  census sheet and count up the total numbers of vehicles.

RESOURCES AND EQUIPMENT

You will find the following resources and equipment useful.
Your teacher should be able to advise you on whether they are
available in school, and your school library or local library will
almost certainly be able to help you.

- **"Fieldwork – First Hand"** by Peter Glynn (Crake hill Press
  1988) ISBN 0 907105 20 3 pages 116 to 118.
- **"Fieldwork"** by Brian Greasley (Bell & Hyman 1984)
  ISBN 0 7135 2675 0 pages 95 to 96 and 127 to 128.
- **"Project Fieldwork"** Fieldwork Investigations 5 by
  Sue Warn (Arnold-Wheaton 1986) ISBN 0 560 06500 0 pages 25
  to 26.
- **"Population and Transport"** Series 2 Issue 3 1979–80 page 5,
  "GEO" magazine
- Local street maps such as those published by the Geographer's
  A-Z Map Company Ltd, Vestry Road, Sevenoaks, Kent, TN14
  5EP or Ordnance Survey 1:1250 scale maps.

7

Other Suggestions from Teachers:

8

GCSE Coursework E...

Reduced example of pages 3 and 4 of Geogr...

margin notes

By now you should have a clear idea of what Human Rights means to you and others. You may have developed your own personal list of *'Rights' priorities* and be working towards their realisation. At the very least you should have understood that Human Rights affects *everyone everywhere.*

How you present your **final report** will be up to you, your teacher and in part be determined by the syllabus you are following. Here are some ideas to consider:

▶ Present everything which you completed in **Activities 1 to 4** in a file. Add an introduction and a conclusion. Large documents might be included as an Appendix.

▶ Arrange a **wall display** of your work.

▶ Take a **lesson** on Human Rights with your class.

▶ Take an **assembly** on Human Rights.

▶ If you did some drama, artwork or music for **Activity 2**, you may like to present it to a wider audience as part of a Human Rights event which you could organise in school for a lunchtime or after school.

11

Presentation : General Hints

However you decide to present your Final Report, you need to make it as informative and interesting as you can.

▶ Aim to maintain interest by variety - this applies whether your presentation is spoken or written.

▶ Use visual aids - newspapers, photographs, diagrams, maps, video presentations - all make a report more interesting.

▶ Label all newspaper cuttings, diagrams, maps carefully and say where they came from.

▶ Remember to include any suggestions for further work that you might have done given the time.

▶ Describe ways in which you might have improved your study and note any problems you faced when completing the coursework.

If you have chosen a written report, **number all pages** and make out a **Contents Page** to put in at the beginning of your report, immediately after your Title Page.

Finally, put in a written 'thank you' *(acknowledgement)* to all the people and organisations who helped you to carry out your investigation.

Go back and check your work - **Be neat, Be careful, Be organised !**

12

> **The Task in Brief**
> Find out about Human Rights
> Decide what you think
> Collect information
> Get involved
> Report

NEP Guides also in Geography & Business Studies   Tel: 0373 - 830833

Reduced example of final page of Humanities Unit 16:
Finding Out About Human Rights

EQUIPMENT NEEDED

- Clipboard
- Paper
- Pencils and Pens
- Watch with a second hand (or digital stopwatch)

PRESENTING YOUR DATA

9

(a) Go back and look at exactly what you are investigating.

(b) Draw a neat version of your tallies, not the totals only, for the four times which you carried out the census.

(c) Write a short description of the situation of the road and its role in the local traffic network. A simple sketch map showing the **methods** which you are investigating and the results.

(d) Write down what you are investigating and which you used.

(e) Draw bar graphs or pie graphs to illustrate the results of your census:

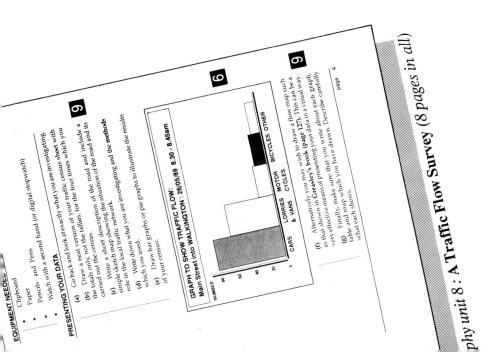

GRAPH TO SHOW TRAFFIC FLOW : 26/05/89 8.30 - 8.45am
Main Street into WALKINGTON

NUMBER: 80, 60, 40, 20, 0

CARS | LORRIES & VANS | MOTOR CYCLES | BICYCLES | OTHER

6

(f) Alternatively you may wish to draw a flow map such (page 127). This can be a visual way. As shown in **Greasley's** book. Write about each graph, very effective means of presenting your data in a visual way. Describe carefully that you have drawn.

(g) Finally, map which you have drawn. table and what each shows.

9

phy unit 8 : A Traffic Flow Survey (8 pages in all)

★ Units 1, 2 & 3 in Geography, and units 1 & 2 in Business Sudies, and Humanities provide valuable advice to both student and teacher in the use of these guides. You are strongly advised to select them.

5 A Share in the Market ☐	16 A Travel Guide to Holidays ☐	27 Industrial Relations ☐
6 Tele-Communications ☐	17 Financial Help(Small Firms) ☐	28 Communications at Work ☐
7 The Planning Question ☐	18 Overseas Trade ☐	29 European Community 1992 ☐
8 Business and Environment ☐	19 Marketing a Product ☐	30 Trading, Profit & Loss, & Balance Sheets ☐
9 Business Computing ☐	20 Investigating the Job Market ☐	31 Break Even Analysis ☐
10 Public / Private Transport ? ☐	21 Personal Budgeting ☐	32 Which Bank To Choose ☐
11 The Cost of Distribution ☐	22 Borrowing Money ☐	

Name _____ Position _____ Institution _____

Address _____ LEA or Borough _____

Order Number _____ Signature _____

_____ Full set(s) of **all 3 subjects** @ discount price of £95 (+£5.00 p+p)

_____ Full set(s) of _____(specify subject/s) @ £35 each (+£2.60 p+p)

_____ pack(s) of **any 5 titles** from any of the 3 subjects @ £10 (+£1.30 p+p)

TOTAL

These prices, the first increase for 18 months, are guaranteed until 31st August 1991. The Company reserves the right to increase postal charges in line with any national rise in postal rates.

Many LEA's and TVEI Groups have made bulk orders at discount rates. Further details on request.

5% off invoice total if cheque is sent with order, payable to *Network Educational Press*

Orders to:

NETWORK EDUCATIONAL PRESS

P.O. Box 635 Stafford ST18 OLJ Telephone: 0889 271300

Please photocopy the order form if you wish to keep this brochure intact

COURSEWORK ENQUIRY/ STUDY GUIDES

A SERIES OF PHOTOCOPIABLE RESOURCE PACKS

The Guides will improve the range and quality of GCSE, Standard Grade and General Studies Coursework and will provide for:

▼ **Flexible Learning**

NETWORK EDUCATIONAL PRESS

1. Wide range of Titles in each Subject.

2. Involvement with local Business and the Community.

3. Clearly defined Aims.

4. Space for notes negotiated between Teacher and Student.

5. Interesting Activities and Fieldwork.

6. Models to follow (graphs, tables, data recording sheets).

7. Useful advice on Resources, People to contact, Places to visit.

The Guides are flexible enough for Class, Group or Individual use

---

GCSE Coursework Enquiry Guide

Geography : 8

A TRAFFIC FLOW SURVEY

Neil Punnett, Wilberforce College, Hull

GCSE Coursework Enquiry Guide

Humanities : 16

FINDING OUT ABOUT HUMAN RIGHTS

Peter Coates, Colfox School, Bridport

GCSE Coursework Enquiry Guide

Business Studies : 13

Planning for Changes in the Workforce

Kate Balfour, St. Bede's School, Bristol

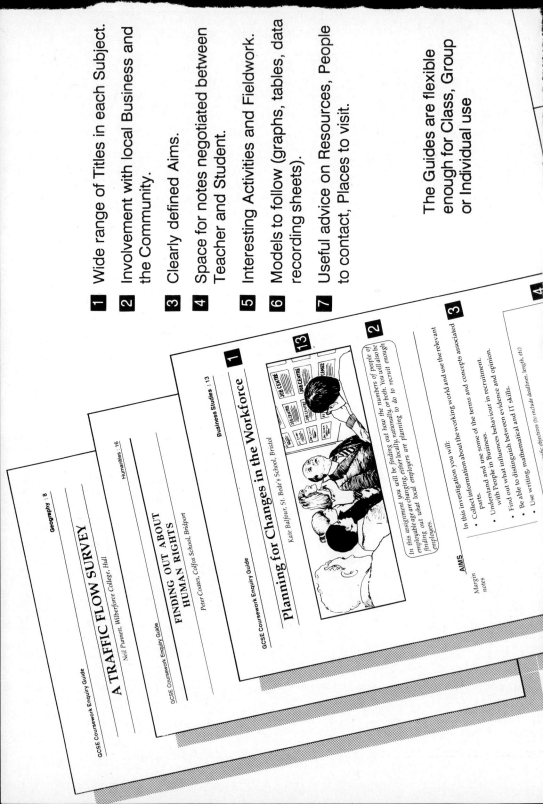

13

In this assignment you will be finding out how the numbers of people of employable age are changing, either locally, nationally, or both. You will also be finding out what local employers are planning to do to recruit enough employees.

2

AIMS   In this investigation you will:

Margin notes

- Collect information about the working world and use the relevant parts.
- Understand and use some of the terms and concepts associated parts.
- Understand and use People in Business.
- Understand People in Business behaviour in recruitment.
- Find out what influences behaviour in recruitment and opinion.
- Find out what influences evidence and opinion.
- Be able to distinguish between evidence and opinion.
- Be able to distinguish mathematical and IT skills.
- Use writing, mathematical and IT skills.

3

- Use writing, mathematical and IT skills.

...fic objectives (to include deadlines, length, etc)

4

All Guides are written by experienced teachers, many of whom
are currently Examiners or Moderators for the GCSE Boards.

8 Space for additional suggestions
from Teacher (videos, local names
addresses etc).

9 Clear, practical advice on sorting and
using information.

10 Active learning, Role play.

11 Advice on the Structuring and
Presentation of Final Report.

12 Hints that improve grades !

13 Attractive illustrations.

...spapers carry articles about merger

...o not have a newspaper with this type of information in it,
...en your local and school / college library will have newspapers
you can look at. **"The Economist"** has articles on mergers and this
will also be available in a library. Many Business Studies and
Economics text books have information on merger activity and
the reasons for it taking place.

The Banks publish quarterly reviews which have information on
merger activities. Your local library may have copies, if not
contact the banks.

Activities

You work in the finance department of a large company.

The **Managing Director** has recently become worried by the large
number of **mergers** and **takeovers** which have been occurring.

You have been **asked** to compile a report covering a number of areas:

Activity 1

Investigate the reasons for mergers and takeovers. Your text book
and many articles in reviews will give you this information. **10**

Activity 2

Conduct a survey of merger activity.

Look back in newspapers to survey the type of **mergers** that have
been taking place.

You could categorise them into the following types:

Whether they were friendly or not.

What type of **industries** they were in.

If the companies involved were **British** or foreign.

Your newspaper cuttings should be neatly presented in a folder
with each article dated.

There might be other areas you would like to include.

Activity 3

Investigate the actions a company could take if it did not want to
merge.

Network Educational Press

Reduced example of page 2 of Business Studies Unit
25: **Mergers and Competition Policy**

Order Form

Please tick choices.

Geography/General Studies/PSE

ISBN 1 85539 000 0

- ★ 1 Introduction: Supporting Independent Learning
- ★ 2 A Model For Coursework
- ★ 3 Interviews & Questionnaires
- 4 River / Stream Study
- 5 Housing and Environment
- 6 Two Shopping Centres
- 7 Town Centre Study
- 8 Traffic Flow Survey
- 9 Village Study
- 10 Quarries & Environment
- 11 Vegetation Study
- 12 Nuclear Energy
- 13 A Local Development
- 14 Residential Environments
- 15 Stream Ordering
- 16 Sports Centre Study
- 17 Changing Holiday Habits
- 18 A Local River Flooding
- 19 Conifer Plantations
- 20 Urban Land Use
- 21 Shopping Centre (1)
- 22 Shopping Centre (2)
- 23 Shopping Centre (3)
- 24 Quality of a Beach
- 25 Seaside Tourism
- 26 House Price Survey
- 27 River Pollution
- 28 Locating a Factory
- 29 Microclimate Study
- 30 World Inequalities
- 31 Traffic Problems
- 32 Impact of a Superstore

Humanities/English/General Studies/PSE

ISBN 1 85539 001 9

- ★ 1 As per Geography (above)
- ★ 2 Interviews & Questionnaires
- 3 Planning Leisure Facilities
- 4 Shopping Trends
- 5 Gender Role Stereotyping
- 6 Our View of the World?
- 7 Industrialisation in Britain
- 8 Media - Seeing isn't always believing
- 9 Young People & Television
- 10 Conservation (Urban Areas)
- 11 Alternative Energy
- 12 Investigate Local Pollution
- 13 Family Change
- 14 Beliefs & Environment
- 15 An Election Role-Play
- 16 Human Rights
- 17 Young Offenders
- 18 Provisions for the Elderly
- 19 Holiday Location
- 20 Interdependence
- 21 Rites of Passage
- 22 Facilities & Phys.Disabled
- 23 "Jokes" and Minority Groups
- 24 Making the most of Work Experience
- 25 Causes of Conflict
- 26 "A Thing of Beauty is a Joy Forever"
- 27 Changing Eating Habits
- 28 Lyrics with a Message
- 29 A Local Political Issue
- 30 Conservation and pollution in the Media

Business Studies/Economic awareness/General Studies/PSE

ISBN 1 85539 002 7

- ★ 1 As per Geography (above)
- ★ 2 Interviews & Questionnaires
- 3 Business Locations
- 4 Advertising: TV v Radio
- 12 Insurance - A Case Study
- 13 Changes in the Workforce
- 14 Health, Safety in the Office
- 15 The Personnel Department
- 23 The Cost of Credit
- 24 Market Research
- 25 Mergers and Competition
- 26 Recruitment

NETWORK
EDUCATIONAL
PRESS

COURSEWORK ENQUIRY/
STUDY GUIDES

A SERIES OF PHOTOCOPIABLE RESOURCE PACKS

The Guides will improve the range and quality of GCSE, Standard Grade
and General Studies Coursework and will provide for :

▼ Flexible Learning

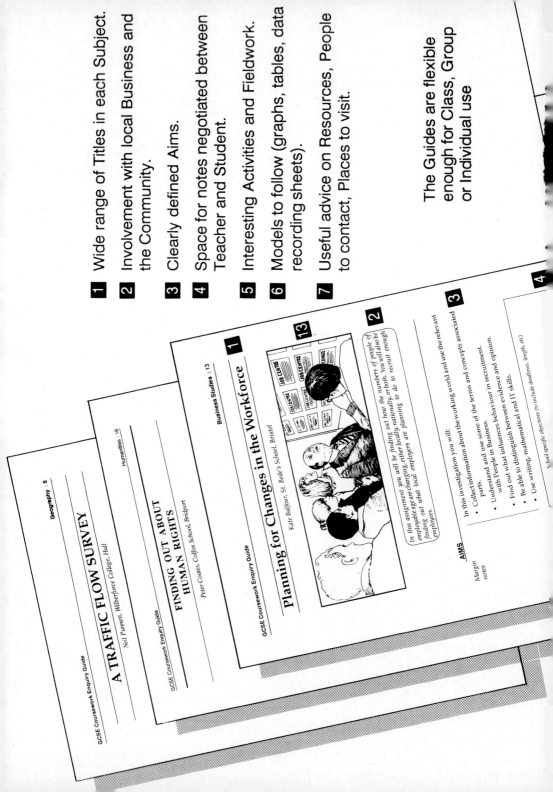

1. Wide range of Titles in each Subject.
2. Involvement with local Business and the Community.
3. Clearly defined Aims.
4. Space for notes negotiated between Teacher and Student.
5. Interesting Activities and Fieldwork.
6. Models to follow (graphs, tables, data recording sheets).
7. Useful advice on Resources, People to contact, Places to visit.

The Guides are flexible enough for Class, Group or Individual use

---

Geography : 8

GCSE Coursework Enquiry Guide

A TRAFFIC FLOW SURVEY

Neil Punnett, Wilberforce College, Hull

Humanities : 16

GCSE Coursework Enquiry Guide

FINDING OUT ABOUT HUMAN RIGHTS

Peter Coates, Colfox School, Bridport

Business Studies : 13

13

GCSE Coursework Enquiry Guide

1

Planning for Changes in the Workforce

Kate Balfour, St. Bede's School, Bristol

In this assignment you will be finding out how the numbers of people of employable age are changing, either locally, nationally, or both. You will also be finding out what local employers are planning to do to recruit enough employees.

2

Margin notes

AIMS

3

In this investigation about the working world and use the relevant associated

In this investigation you will:

- Collect information about the working world and use the relevant parts.
- Understand and use some of the terms and concepts associated with People in Business.
- Understand and use People in Business behaviour in recruitment.
- Find out what influences behaviour and opinion.
- Be able to distinguish between evidence and opinion.
- Use writing, mathematical and IT skills.

school specific objectives (to include deadlines, length, etc)

4

All Guides are written by experienced teachers, many of whom are currently Examiners or Moderators for the GCSE Boards.

8 Space for additional suggestions from Teacher (videos, local names addresses etc).

9 Clear, practical advice on sorting and using information.

10 Active learning, Role play.

11 Advice on the Structuring and Presentation of Final Report.

12 Hints that improve grades !

13 Attractive illustrations.

ry Guide

Geography : 8

Business Studies : 25

...spapers carry articles about merger

...o not have a newspaper with this type of information in it, ...uen your local and school / college library will have newspapers you can look at **"The Economist"** has articles on mergers and this will also be available in a library. Many Business Studies and Economics text books have information on merger activity and the reasons for it taking place.

The Banks publish quarterly reviews which have information on merger activities. Your local library may have copies, if not contact the banks.

Activities

You work in the finance department of a large company.

The **Managing Director** has recently become worried by the large number of **mergers** and **takeovers** which have been occurring.

You have been **asked** to compile a report covering a number of areas:

Activity 1

Investigate the reasons for mergers and takeovers. Your text book and many articles in reviews will give you this information.

Activity 2

Conduct a survey of merger activity.

Look back in newspapers to survey the type of **mergers** that have been taking place.

You could categorise them into the following types:

Whether they were friendly or not.

What type of **industries** they were in.

If the companies involved were **British** or foreign.

Your newspaper cuttings should be neatly presented in a folder with each article dated.

There might be other areas you would like to include.

Activity 3

Investigate the actions a company could take if it did not want to **merge**.

10

page 2

Network Educational Press

Reduced example of page 2 of Business Studies Unit 25: **Mergers and Competition Policy**

Please tick choices.

Order Form

Geography/General Studies/PSE

- ★ 1 Introduction: Supporting Independent Learning
- ★ 2 A Model For Coursework
- ★ 3 Interviews & Questionnaires
- ★ 4 River / Stream Study
- 5 Housing and Environment
- 6 Two Shopping Centres
- 7 Town Centre Study
- 8 Traffic Flow Survey
- 9 Village Study
- 10 Quarries & Environment
- 11 Vegetation Study
- 12 Nuclear Energy
- 13 A Local Development
- 14 Residential Environments
- 15 Stream Ordering
- 16 Sports Centre Study
- 17 Changing Holiday Habits
- 18 A Local River Flooding
- 19 Conifer Plantations
- 20 Urban Land Use
- 21 Shopping Centre (1)

ISBN 1 85539 000 0
- 22 Shopping Centre (2)
- 23 Shopping Centre (3)
- 24 Quality of a Beach
- 25 Seaside Tourism
- 26 House Price Survey
- 27 River Pollution
- 28 Locating a Factory
- 29 Microclimate Study
- 30 World Inequalities
- 31 Traffic Problems
- 32 Impact of a Superstore

Humanities/English/General Studies/PSE

- ★ 1 As per Geography (above)
- ★ 2 Interviews & Questionnaires
- 3 Planning Leisure Facilities
- 4 Shopping Trends
- 5 Gender Role Stereotyping
- 6 Our View of the World?
- 7 Industrialisation in Britain
- 8 Media - Seeing isn't always believing
- 9 Young People & Television
- 10 Conservation (Urban Areas)
- 11 Alternative Energy
- 12 Investigate Local Pollution
- 13 Family Change
- 14 Beliefs & Environment
- 15 An Election Role-Play
- 16 Human Rights
- 17 Young Offenders
- 18 Provisions for the Elderly
- 19 Holiday Location
- 20 Interdependence
- 21 Rites of Passage

ISBN 1 85539 001 9
- 22 Facilities & Phys.Disabled
- 23 "Jokes" and Minority Groups
- 24 Making the most of Work Experience
- 25 Causes of Conflict
- 26 "A Thing of Beauty is a Joy Forever"
- 27 Changing Eating Habits
- 28 Lyrics with a Message
- 29 A Local Political Issue
- 30 Conservation and pollution in the Media

Business Studies/Economic awareness/General Studies/PSE

- ★ 1 As per Geography (above)
- ★ 2 Interviews & Questionnaires
- 3 Business Locations
- 4 Advertising: TV v Radio
- 12 Insurance - A Case Study
- 13 Changes in the Workforce
- 14 Health, Safety in the Office
- 15 The Personnel Department

ISBN 1 85539 002 7
- 23 The Cost of Credit
- 24 Market Research
- 25 Mergers and Competition
- 26 Recruitment

▼ **Supported Self-Study**

▼ **Active Learning**

▼ **Links with the Community**

▼ **90 different titles**

An Introduction written by

PHILIP WATERHOUSE

provides advice on how these guides can be used for
whole class, group or independent learning.

5 A Share in the Market	16 A Travel Guide to Holidays	27 Industrial Relations
6 Tele-Communications	17 Financial Help(Small Firms)	28 Communications at Work
7 The Planning Question	18 Overseas Trade	29 European Community 1992
8 Business and Environment	19 Marketing a Product	30 Trading, Profit & Loss, & Balance Sheets
9 Business Computing	20 Investigating the Job Market	31 Break Even Analysis
10 Public / Private Transport ?	21 Personal Budgeting	32 Which Bank To Choose
11 The Cost of Distribution	22 Borrowing Money	

★ Units 1,2 & 3 in Geography, and units 1 & 2 in Business Sudies. and Humanities provide valuable advice to both student and teacher in the use of these guides. You are strongly advised to select them.

Name _____ Position _____ Institution _____

Address _____

LEA or Borough _____

Order Number _____ Signature _____

_____ Full set(s) of **all 3 subjects** @ discount price of £95 (+£5.00 p+p)

_____ Full set(s) of _____ (specify subject/s) @ £35 each (+£2.60 p+p)

_____ pack(s) of **any 5 titles** from any of the 3 subjects @ £10 (+£1.30 p+p)

TOTAL

These prices, the first increase for 18 months, are guaranteed until 31st August 1991. The Company reserves the right to increase postal charges in line with any national rise in postal rates.

Many LEA's and TVEI Groups have made bulk orders at discount rates. Further details on request.

5% off invoice total if cheque is sent with order, payable to *Network Educational Press*
Orders to:

NETWORK EDUCATIONAL PRESS
P.O. Box 635 Stafford ST18 OLJ Telephone: **0889 271300**

Please photocopy the order form if you wish to keep this brochure intact

5

Flexible Learning and the Curriculum

Flexible Learning and the
National Curriculum
Changes for the 16−19 Group
The Curriculum Within Institutions

FLEXIBLE LEARNING AND THE CURRICULUM

In what ways do the aims and the structure of the curriculum contribute towards more flexible ways of learning? The question needs to be addressed at two levels: the national level because this is where the major decisions about the aims and structures are now being made; and the institutional level at which the detailed organisation is being done.

A   ## Flexible Learning and the National Curriculum

Some general points

Teachers view the national curriculum with a certain amount of anxiety. Will it impose a rigid structure and will it set targets that will force them to abandon flexible ways of working with their students? Will it prescribe programmes of study in such detail that they will lose all their sense of ownership of what they were doing? Will they have to spend a disproportionate amount of their time in testing for the national curriculum? This anxieties are natural enough given the speed at which the changes have been introduced.

We can try to answer these questions now because the students who have recently entered the secondary school are already working, at least partly, within the framework of the national curriculum. Over the next few years this will be rapidly extended. The proposals are now available in *mathematics, science, english, geography, history,*and in *design and technology*. A style and a pattern are already emerging and it is possible to form views about the likely answers to the teachers' burning questions.

For each foundation subject of the national curriculum the Education Reform Act defines:

- **appropriate attainment targets** (ie. the knowledge, skills and understanding which pupils of different abilities and maturities are expected to have by the end of each key stage)
- **programmes of study** (ie. the matters, skills and processes which are required to be taught to pupils of different abilities and maturities during each key stage)
- **assessment arrangements**

Details of the assessment arrangements have not yet been finalised. But attainment targets and programmes of study are available (some still at the proposal stage) and teachers have been studying them carefully. They have been concerned for the development of the whole pupil. Will the proposals squeeze out the development of those personal and social qualities which help students on the road to maturity? Will some of the best methods and styles have to be abandoned? Many teachers will have been pleasantly reassured with what they have found. The national curriculum is certainly demanding with regard to knowledge and understanding, and most teachers would not quarrel with that. But it addresses itself also to **flexible methods of learning.** In doing so it doesn't merely allow them; in many areas it is actually **demanding them.**

Science in the national curriculum

A more detailed examination of the Orders now being implemented in science will illustrate the point.

Attainment target 1: Exploration of science

Pupils should develop the intellectual and practical skills that allow them to explore the world of science and to develop a fuller understanding of scientific phenomena and the procedures of scientific exploration and investigation. This work should take place in the context of activities that require a progressively more systematic and quantified approach, which draws upon an increasing knowledge and understanding of science. The activities should encourage the ability to:

i.   plan, hypothesise and predict

ii.   design and carry out investigations

iii.   interpret results and findings

iv.   draw inferences

v.   communicate exploratory tasks and experiments.

(Science in the National Curriculum. HMSO. 1989)

These are general skills, which are as much concerned with the processes of learning as with the content of the subject. They imply intellectual and practical activity going on simultaneously and mutually supportive. They paint a picture of cooperation, of deliberation and communication. They imply much talk, and talk at a high intellectual level. These kind of targets simply cannot be reached through didactic teaching. They are the stuff of **flexible learning.**

This first attainment target *(AT1 - Exploration in Science)* has been given a weighting of 35% for the *key stage 3 (11-14 year olds)*, the other 65% being allocated to the remaining 16 targets. This is a very strong emphasis indeed.

An examination of the prescribed programmes of study is equally reassuring. In the general introduction to the *key stage 4 (14-16 years)* programme the following note on communication is prominent:

> Pupils should be given the opportunities further to develop their skills of reporting and recording. They should be encouraged to articulate their own ideas and work independently or contribute to group efforts. They should develop research skills through selecting and using reference materials and through gathering and organising information from a number of sources and perspectives. They should have the opportunity to translate information from one form to another to suit audience and purpose and to use databases and spreadsheets in their work.

(Science in the National Curriculum. HMSO. 1989)

Quite apart from the encouragement of the attainment targets and the programmes of study, the Order laid before parliament is very encouraging. **It makes no demands on how much time is to be allocated to the subject, on how it is to be timetabled, or how it is to be organised - separate subjects, integrated, combined, or modular.** It also allows flexibility for teaching outside the ranges of levels specified where it seems in the interests of an individual pupil. This is altogether reassuring and should, in the long run, strengthen the development of flexible learning in science.

Some evidence from the proposals for English

The pattern and style of the science order is mirrored in the proposals made for other subjects.

In the consultations for the English proposals there has been some debate about the relative importance to be attached to **speaking** and **listening.** Many professionals have reflected the views expressed by HMI that these skills have been neglected and that the national curriculum provides an opportunity for a better balance to be struck. This viewpoint has been strongly supported by a number of interested groups representing industry and business. The following quote was given prominence in the original proposal.

Where children are given responsibility they are placed in situations where it becomes important for them to communicate - to discuss, to negotiate, to converse - with their fellows, with the staff, with other adults. And of necessity they are likely to develop oral skills. This basically is how oracy grows: it is to be taught by the creation of many and varied circumstances to which both speech and listening are the natural responses.

(Spoken English. Educational Review. Occasional Publications No. 2. University of Birmingham. 1985.)

So speaking and listening form a separate profile component in the English proposal, an indication that the working party regarded them as vitally important in young people's development. The importance of **group work** is also recognised in the National Curriculum guidelines.

In order to achieve **level 7,** pupils should participate extensively in widely varied group work in a range of groupings. They should be encouraged to take on an increasingly responsible role, *eg. by taking notes of the discussion and checking them with the group, representing group views in plenary sessions.*

(English in the National Curriculum. HMSO.1990.)

If the spirit of these thoughts is finally implemented it will be of great encouragement to the many English teachers who have emphasised oracy and who have developed skills in using small groups as the basis for learning.

Design and technology in the national curriculum

The proposals for design and technology present an exciting challenge to teachers engaged in those fields. The summary of attainment targets 1-4 is worth quoting in full.

Attainment targets and statements of attainment for design and technology capability

AT1 - *Identifying needs and opportunities*

Pupils should be able to identify and state clearly needs and opportunities for design and technological activities through investigation of the contexts of home, school, recreation, community, business and industry.

AT2 - *Generating a design*

Pupils should be able to generate a design specification, explore ideas to produce a design proposal and develop it into a realistic, appropriate and achievable design.

AT3 - *Planning and making*

Pupils should be able to make artefacts, systems and environments, preparing and working to a plan and identifying, managing and using appropriate resources, including knowledge and processes.

AT4 - *Evaluating*

Pupils should be able to develop, communicate and act upon an evaluation of the processes, products and effects of their design and technological activities and those of others, including those from other times and cultures.

(Technology in the National Curriculum. HMSO. 1990)

Interesting quotes from the Programme of study for key stages 3 and 4 give a feel of the implications for styles of teaching and learning.

> Within the general requirements of design and technology, pupils should have increasing opportunities for more open-ended research, leading to the identification of tasks for designing and making. There should be opportunities for some of these activities to take place outside school.

(Key stage 3)

> Activities should include at least one extended design and technological task, for example with a duration of between 15 and 30 hours. There should be opportunities for visits and work outside school, including work experience placements.

(Key stage 4)

The programmes of study for **information technology** capability include the following points:

> In each key stage pupils should develop information technology capabilities through a range of curriculum activities which will:
>
> ..... encourage the flexibility needed to take advantage of future developments in information technology.....
>
> ..... enable pupils to take greater responsibility for their own learning, and provide opportunities for them to decide when it is appropriate to use information technology in their work.

(Technology in the National Curriculum. HMSO. 1990)

There is a lot more to the proposals and this is not the place to describe them in detail. Yet the implications are great for flexible learning.

- Teachers will have greater demands made on their own flexibility. They are likely to find themselves organising learning across a much broader area than their own subject specialism.

- The targets and programmes are aimed at students of all abilities. There will be big changes for schools that have previously distinguished between design and technology for older and abler students and craft subjects for younger and less able students.

- **A major in-service training programme will be required.** Teachers will become managers of the learning process, using all the managerial techniques. The skills involved are personal and social, and these need to be developed in support of and in association with the knowledge and skills of the subject matter itself. It is impossible to envisage successful implementation of the national curriculum in design and technology **without skilful use of the techniques and styles of flexible learning.**

These three short discussions from the national curriculum proposals in *science, english,* and *design and technology* were intended to demonstrate the significance of the national curriculum for flexible learning.

Of course many teachers at the present stage are probably conscious of the burden of the proposals. The amount of work involved is considerable. However the long term effect is undoubtedly going to be as the government originally wished - to ensure breadth and balance in the school curriculum. When the initial work involved in the re-structuring of school curricula has been accomplished the teachers will be able to devote all their energies to the methods, styles and techniques for delivery. This is professional work of a very high order, and it is right that teachers should be given the necessary time and the right amount of discretion in order to accomplish it properly.

B   ## Changes for the 16 - 19 age group

During the last two years there has been growing dissatisfaction with the
16 - 19 curriculum. Teachers have contrasted the improvements brought
about through the GCSE with the slower pace of progress in A-levels.
There has been concern about breadth and balance, and about the barrier
that exists between the academic routes and the vocational. Recent
proposals from the government may help to resolve these difficulties
and come to the aid of those individual teachers, institutions, and
development projects where attempts are being made to unblock the
system.

The broad intentions of the proposals (not yet worked out in detail) are
as follows.

- All vocational and academic courses post-16 will include a core
  of compulsory studies.

- The core will include communications, information technology,
  numeracy, and modern foreign languages.

- Vocational courses will be more widely available in the schools.

- Students will be able to accumulate credits and take them with
  them whenever they switch courses or institutions.

- School leavers will be given vouchers which will entitle them to
  off-the-job training after they have left full-time education.

These proposals represent a significant move in the direction of a
broader curriculum and a more flexible approach to the management of
the education of this age group.

- Post-16 education will become a much more attractive
  proposition. *Staying on* rates could be significantly improved.

- With a modular organisation it should be possible to transfer
  credits obtained on short vocational courses into the coursework
  requirements of A-level subjects.

- Total transfer from an academic course to a vocational course,
  and vice versa, should be much easier.

The immediate questions for school will be concerned with staffing and
timetables. How can it all be accomplished with problems of
recruitment and with the time pressures on schools?

 It will all strengthen the case for more flexible ways of delivering the
curriculum.

- Teachers may have to question the amount of 'contact time' needed for this age group.
- They will almost certainly need to give more attention to those styles and techniques which promote and depend on a rapidly developing sense of student responsibility.

C   The curriculum within institutions

OVERALL MANAGEMENT OF THE CURRICULUM

The national curriculum together with other government initiatives have certainly not removed the need for the management of the curriculum at school level. At first a lot of time will have to be spent on getting to grips with the requirements of the national curriculum, and keeping up to date as changes are introduced. But it is to be hoped that schools will eventually find that they are able to switch their own efforts. They will be able to concentrate more on the **development** of the national curriculum building on the firm foundations that are being provided. There is likely to be a shift in emphasis in schemes of work from **what** is being offered (because it will have already been defined), to **how** the curriculum is to be presented and delivered. Some considerations for individual institutions follow.

The departmental structure

The departmental structure is still used by the majority of schools for the delivery of the curriculum. At its best it is influential and effective. There is no reason why this strong tradition cannot prove equal to the demanding tasks set by the national curriculum. It all comes down to flexibility and some points for consideration are offered. This could be a wiser course than hastily setting up new and untried structures - management by assimilation rather than management by accretion! But flexibility must be the order of the day.

The process of curriculum development

Adapting to national initiatives

Below are some suggestions for action which may help departments to operate in the more flexible ways which the national curriculum is demanding. (Of course, some departments will already be working in these ways.)

- Extend or modify the job description of the head of department to take into account the needs of the national curriculum.

- Start **now** the practice of working in partnership with other departments to establish links and shared areas of work. Start with small schemes in order to gain confidence and experience in working together.
- Carry out similar cooperative projects with contributory primary schools. Again, start modestly.
- Carry out a review of the department's scheme of work with a view to **(a)** adapting it to the requirements of the national curriculum (when known), and **(b)** designing it as an extension of the national curriculum statement concentrating on resources, teaching methods, differentiation, recording of progress. HMI have consistently claimed that one of the significant indicators of a successful department is the extent to which its scheme of work tackles these issues.

The processes of development and improvement

If the subject department is to be the main vehicle for the delivery of the new curriculum it must be strong enough and capable. It must have leadership of high quality. **The professional development of the middle managers of schools has never been as important as now.** We need people who have a naturally collaborative style, are skilled communicators, and who have a global vision of the purposes of education and the objectives of the school.

They need to be encouraged to set up regular and honest reviews of the work of their departments using all the support that can be obtained from the senior management of the school and from the local authority's advisory and inspection services.

ISSUES FOR LOCAL DECISION

With the broad pattern of foundation subjects already prescribed the individual school will be able to concentrate its major decision-making on a smaller number of issues.

Important cross-curricular themes

The national curriculum determines the subjects that must comprise the bulk of the school curriculum, but does not prescribe how the school day should be organised and the curriculum delivered. Schools have always recognised that there are a number of subject areas and themes which do not fit neatly within the existing framework of subjects and departmental organisation. They have wished to respond to these needs especially where a theme has been identified as a major area for concern or community action.

The responses could be through:

- specially designed courses,
- separate contributions of individual subject departments,
- provision made in the general life of the school (often outside the weekly timetable).

Many schools have preferred specially designed courses but they may now find difficulty in allocating sufficient time and will turn instead to the idea of building on the framework laid down by the national curriculum. The consultation document offered guidance.

> Within the programmes of study teachers will be free to determine the detail of what should be taught in order to ensure that pupils achieve appropriate levels of attainment. How teaching is organised and the teaching approaches used will be also for schools to determine. It is proposed that schools should set out schemes of work for teaching at various stages to improve coordination. The government intends that legislation should leave full scope for professional judgment and for schools to organise how the curriculum is delivered in the way best suited to the ages, circumstances, needs and abilities of the children in each classroom. This will for example allow curriculum development programmes such as the Technical and Vocational Education Initiative (TVEI) to build on the framework offered by the national curriculum and to take forward its objectives. There must be space to accommodate the enterprise of teachers, offering them sufficient flexibility in the choice of content to adapt what they teach to the needs of the individual pupil, to try out and develop new approaches, and to develop in pupils those personal qualities which cannot be written into a programme of study or attainment target.

(National Curriculum 5-16 Consultation Document. HMSO 1987)

In *'Secondary Schools: An Appraisal by HMI'*, HMSO 1988, the inspectors looked at the following cross-curricular issues. These are the headings used and the list is simply intended as a check list.

- Health Education
- An Understanding of Industry and Commerce

- ☐ Work Experience
- ☐ Environmental Education
- ☐ Information Technology
- ☐ An Understanding of Multi-Ethnic Society
- ☐ Equal Opportunities for Boys and Girls
- ☐ Personal, Social and Moral Education
- ☐ Careers Education and Guidance

A curriculum for all

Grouping

Schools adopt four broad types of grouping within their main school organisation:

- mixed ability grouping
- banding
- setting
- streaming

What is the significance of each of these from the point of view of flexible learning?

It is important to recognise that the type of grouping in itself does not determine the ways in which young people learn. For example a class may be formed according to some rigid streaming formula, yet the teacher may still feel that flexible learning approaches are desirable, because of the individual differences within the group and because there is intrinsic merit in the more personal and less regimented style.

On the whole however teachers tend to equate mixed ability grouping with more flexible methods because the mixed ability grouping **demands** greater attention to be given to providing varied resources and differentiated tasks.

The most important requirement for flexibility is surely that whatever system is used it should be capable of adapting to changing circumstances and changing individual needs.

- Many schools prefer to divide a year group into a number of equal size 'populations' and to allow subject departments to make decisions about grouping according to the logic of their own situation.

- Departments are encouraged to move students from one group to another whenever the individual's needs seem to justify it.

Differentiation

This is surely one of the most important issues for local decision. Most teachers have readily accepted that it would be wrong for the national curriculum to specify different targets for different students. They have preferred the approach which defines progressive levels of achievement within broad attainment targets, and these are applicable to all. This means that students will be able to progress at the pace that is suitable for them. It does not in any way interfere with the clear age-related standards which are linked with particular levels of achievement.

But teachers are all too aware of the intricate nature of individual differences. The diagram below summarises only the broad headings.

INDIVIDUAL DIFFERENCES

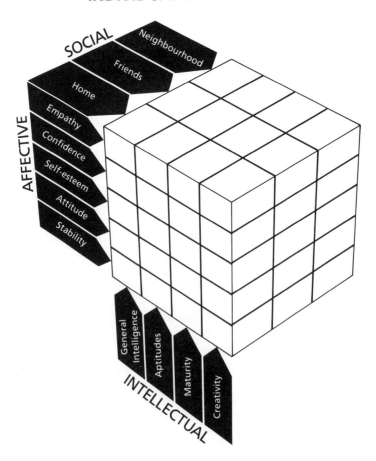

Teachers also know about the wide range of strategies and techniques that are available to them in their response to individual differences. The headings for these are also summarised diagramatically.

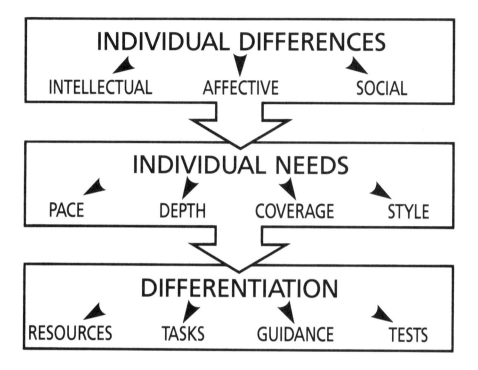

RESPONDING TO INDIVIDUAL DIFFERENCES

The problem is to find effective ways of managing this extremely complex state of affairs. It calls for great flexibility and ingenuity, and teachers are right to call for a massive training programme to give them time to work out effective techniques and to practise the management styles.

This Handbook can only briefly mention the problem of differentiation.

Differentiation is dealt with in some depth in two other books in the series: *Classroom Management* and *Resources for Flexible Learning*. For further details see page 85.

Flexible Methods

Counselling and Guidance

Individual Action Plans

Study Skills Training

Active Learning Techniques

Independent Learning

Tutorial Support

Use of Library

Management of Private Study

Use of Technology

FLEXIBLE METHODS

At the end of the day, all the planning, all the discussion, all the elaborate structures, attainment targets and programmes of study will count for nothing if there is no **inspiration** at the points where teachers and learners meet. If there is no **imagination** and **flexibility** in the classroom then curriculum planning is a paper exercise.

Education is about the experiences of the learner. So it is right that much thought and effort in flexible learning has been directed at the ways in which teaching and learning is organised. Most teachers would agree with these broad statements of principle.

- Educational methods which seek to promote the growing responsibility of the learner ought to emphasise the learner's activity and involvement.

- Learners should experience a broad repertoire of teaching and learning styles. This gives them the opportunity to work in a variety of ways and to appreciate that greater knowledge, understanding and capability can be reached via many different routes. Much of the success in an education comes about through becoming a good *route-finder.*

- Every opportunity should be taken to adapt the learning programmes to the abilities, interests and learning styles of individuals. Balancing this with the previous principle is part of the skill of teaching. Learners must have their individual personalities respected, but at the same time, the job of an educator is to help them to expand their repertoires. **Getting this balance just right is an important professional responsibility.**

Flexibility can manifest itself in many teaching and learning situations. It is important to recognise that mere titles for learning activities can mean little. It is what actually happens in the experience of the learners that counts. For example a lesson devoted to **'class teaching'** could be organised in a flexible and participative style with input from the teacher nicely punctuated with individual or small group tasks in order to give the students a strong sense of involvement. Conversely a lesson devoted to **'independent study'** could be a dreary trudge through a succession of monotonous worksheets which give no scope for decision making or personal contribution. **The names we give to our teaching methods can be misleading!**

Here are a number of activities which seem to offer good prospects for putting the principles of flexible learning into practice. Again, in keeping with the *Outline* objectives of this handbook, only a brief introduction is offered for each one in turn. It is in other handbooks in the series that the full range of possibilities for the method will be discussed.

A Counselling and guidance

Counselling and guidance is a feature of all secondary schools today. The need is great, and probably greater than is provided in most schools. There have been significant advances in personal counselling, in careers guidance, and in the broader aspects of educational guidance concerned with course choices etc. These matters are often handled in 'tutor time' which is regularly timetabled. Sometimes these same periods are given over to programmes of personal and social education. All this is laudable and undoubtedly improves the quality of school life for many students. Counselling and guidance is a major contribution towards the objectives of flexible learning.

Yet it is still common to hear complaints of time being allocated as *'tutor time'* with the teachers uncertain as to how best to use the time. There is a strong case for much more individual guidance to be offered to students in a more detailed way and this is discussed in the next section.

B Individual action plans

The idea of *individual action plans* is a valuable one. The idea can work well in thinking about long-term plans and this is encouraged in many schools. But it is often more effective if students learn first how to work to short term plans. They need experience in talking about this week's work - problems of *organisation, workload, resources* and *facilities*. They need to learn the technique of setting themselves objectives of a general nature to guide all their work over a short period of time. This is something which can be offered over and above the guidance and support that the students receive from their subject teachers. Teachers do not always realise the level of their own expertise in matters concerning the organisation and skills of studying. Some students have always had this kind of support from wise and experienced parents; we should offer it to all of them.

It is the simple logistics of the operation which seem to present most difficulties. How does a form tutor, allocated a short amount of time each week, cover all the counselling and guidance needs of a class of students **and** succeed in helping each one to design useful individual action plans?

It would be a hopeless task for a teacher working alone. But a school can make it possible by concentrating some effort in three broad directions:

1) Providing resources to support **independent** learning within the areas of counselling and guidance. There are many published schemes which will help teachers to organise the learning in this way. Working independently benefits the students of course, but it also helps the teacher by usefully occupying a group of students while others are being tutored.

2) Providing training for teachers in the techniques of **small-group tutorial work**. It may seem to be a contradiction to imply that individual action plans should be made through work in small groups. However there is much experience to suggest that this is the best way to do it. And it is the only really effective way from the point of view of the teacher's own time. A well organised tutorial, thoroughly involving all the students, can result in well-designed action plans for each individual and a valuable experience of collaboration and mutual support.

3) Exploring **timetable arrangements** which will enable teachers to fulfil their roles in counselling and guidance. Some schools have carefully timetabled tutorial time so that form tutors, at least for some of their allocated time, have smaller groups for the making of individual action plans.

Of course well organised individual action plans cannot be brought into existence overnight. They are invariably the product of a carefully sustained development programme, involving the collaboration of all the staff of a school. They demand:

- the careful management of time (by senior management in the timetable, and by teachers within the timetable)
- a sensitive approach to tutoring.

C   Study skills training

The development of study skills is bound to help in the progressive training towards greater responsibility in learning. However there are some possible pitfalls.

It is unwise to **teach** study skills separately from the main tasks of learning. When students are taught courses of study skills in this way they often fail to discover the personal relevance for themselves. They often do not succeed in transferring the messages of the lessons into their real studies.

Study skills are best learned on the job. A useful definition of a skill will help explain this idea. A skill is the ability to perform a useful task to a high standard, **without necessarily being able to explain the rules that govern that high performance**. So it is **experience** and **practice** that really counts. But this doesn't preclude two kinds of support from the teacher - personal counselling; and some coaching in the skills themselves **when the need arises.** The diagram overleaf explains this view of study skills.

It is important too to emphasise that study skills must go well beyond simple techniques and study 'tips'. Students need help at the strategic level throughout all their work.

The implication of this is that study skills are the concern of the whole teaching staff. Every teacher is a teacher of study skills. This will be reassuring for many subject specialists who feel that the methods and skills in their subjects are specific to the subject or need to be developed in particular ways.

So study skills could appear on the school's overall plan like this.

1) There is a teacher with overall responsibility who is mainly concerned with coordination, cross-curricular issues, and staff development.

2) Subject teachers assume responsibility for making contributions to the whole school policy for study skills through their subject teaching.

3) Form tutors, librarians, and all teachers when acting in general support roles accept their responsibility for tutorial support focusing on learning techniques and strategies.

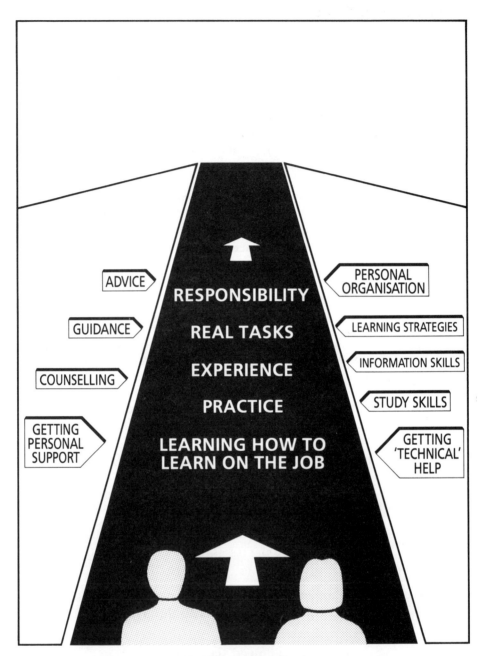

A VIEW OF STUDY SKILLS

D   ## Active learning techniques

The term *active learning* covers a wide range of methods and techniques. The basic characteristics are:

- ☐   an emphasis on learning by doing

- ☐   an emphasis on student decision making

Without discussion in any detail here is a checklist of methods and techniques. The point about many of them is that they simply provide an agenda or a procedure which ensures activity by each member and avoids the chaos which can sometimes result if group discussion or activity is invited without any guidance as to how to proceed.

- **Mini-lectures** - prepared and given by individual students.

- **Debates** - groups are formed to prepare and present opposing views.

- **Coaching** - a learner is challenged to help another learner to achieve a high standard in some knowledge or skill.

- **Rehearsing** - a learner or group practises a particular piece of learning until mastery is claimed.

- **Rounds** - a way of making sure that everyone in a small group takes an active part. For example, when a group is asked to identify problems, do it by a round rather than a brainstorm.

- **Problem solving** - each student in a group identifies a problem or a question, writes it down and passes it to the next student. A short time is allowed for reflection and then each student in turn is asked to explain to the group his/her problem and to go as far as possible in answering it.

- **Reviewing** - a piece of work that has been done independently is reviewed by another student. This occasionally replaces the student himself or the teacher doing the review. You need to make sure that the work is handed over in plenty of time for the reviewing student to study it.

- **Team assessment** - with a class organised in teams, the sum of the marks obtained by individuals within a team is given prominence. So teams are competing against each other. Within the team mutual aid is allowed, and there is a strong incentive to give and ask for support.

It is possible to extend this list considerably, and this is done in the **Handbook of Classroom Management** which is part of this series.

But it is well worthwhile for a subject department in a school to build up its own checklist of active learning techniques which have proved useful for individual teachers. Thinking up these approaches and techniques requires only two questions. What will the students actually do? What decisions will be demanded of the students? The aim is to increase the amount of student activity and decision making to as high a level as possible.

E   Independent learning

Most students can work independently of the teacher. For some this can only work for very short periods measured in minutes; for others it can be for much longer periods measured in hours or even days.

A lot depends on how the process is managed and supported and many of the methods described in this chapter are about *management* and *support*. In this section we simply list the activities which seem to lend themselves well to independent learning without concerning ourselves about how they are managed and supported.

- □ **Conventional learning tasks.**
  This is the only one that requires some explanation. It simply means expecting the students to tackle a topic within a syllabus independently of the teacher. It is the most straightforward of independent learning tasks, but is often under-used because teachers assume that independent learning has to be vastly different from normal work involving new locations and complex resource arrangements. It is the easiest independent learning to organise because it can be done with the resources that are already available. It should be used much more because of the valuable experience it gives without too much of an additional administrative burden.

- □ Projects.

- □ Library research.

- □ Community work.

- □ Work experience.

- □ Mini-enterprises.

- □ Private study and Homework.

- □ Coursework.

- □ General Studies.

F ## Tutorial Support

Tutorial support is the most powerful way of helping students to cope with taking on more responsibility for their own learning. It is such an important topic that a whole handbook in this series is devoted to it. An outline of the main ideas of tutoring now follows.

☐ **Reasons for tutoring**

Young learners are not ready to 'fly solo'. They need a great deal of guidance and help, and a firm framework within which to exercise their responsibilities.

☐ **The arrangements for tutoring**

There are strong arguments for tutoring to be arranged in small groups. This is economic in the use of the teacher's time. It is less intimidating for the individual student, and it provides a rich and varied mixture of opinion and action.

☐ **The agenda of the tutorial**

There should be a clear agenda which focuses on a small number of tasks to be performed. The agenda should be known to the students in advance. Possible items include - review, assessment, briefing, contracting, discussion, coaching.

☐ **The educational objectives of the tutorial**

These should be at the forefront of the teacher's mind throughout. They can be concerned with intellectual development, personal relationships, the social benefits, and the managerial requirements.

☐ **The style and techniques of the tutorial**

Full involvement of the students in both action and decision making are desirable. The tutorial is an educational experience in its own right. It is not merely a mechanism for enabling independent learning to take place. It is an opportunity and a challenge for the students to demonstrate their growing capability as autonomous learners.

A separate handbook in the series is devoted to the important issue of Tutoring. For further details see page 86.

G Use of the library

The school library is an essential facility in the arrangements for flexible learning. There is so much to be done to enhance the role of the library and the librarian in schools, but the following points seem to be particularly important in this context:

☐ The library ought to serve almost exclusively the needs of the **individual** student and not be used for other purposes which have the effect of excluding the individual learner. Thinking and planning about library developments should be guided by this principle.

☐ The library should be available throughout the school day and longer if possible. It is also worth exploring the possibility making it available outside the school terms.

☐ The library should be under the control of a responsible person throughout the day.

☐ Seating arrangements should be conducive to **private** study. This means giving attention to the location of study areas and the ways in which the tables and chairs are arranged. The objective is to create a which is not likely to be disturbed by the movements or activities of others.

☐ There should be facilities for accessing sources of information other than books.

☐ Subject departments should cooperate with library staff to ensure that subject resources are available in the library for the use of individual students. This is particularly valuable where the work of the department relies on written assignments which refer to a wide range of resources. Students often welcome the opportunity to consolidate or extend their understanding in private without having to wait for the next lesson to get access to the resources.

☐ There should be well understood procedures to facilitate the use of the library by individual students during lesson times. Some simple documentation can help, not only as an *'admission ticket'*, but also as a short form of contract which provides guidance.

H ## Management of private study

There is a tradition of private study in sixth forms but almost none in the main school. There is also a tradition of complaints about the inability of the sixth formers to organise their private study time effectively. The cause of this is not difficult to identify. Students will not cope unless they are given **progressive training** in study habits and techniques, and the bulk of this training needs to be based on experience and practice **on the job**. The sooner it is started, the better.

The demands of GCSE and Standard Grade have caused many schools to introduce private study time into fourth and fifth year timetables. It would be of great benefit if this trend could be continued into the lower school.

Private study for the students of the main school may seem like a problem. The need for supervision is obvious if more than a handful of students is involved. But it is far better to convert this situation into an opportunity.

We must start from an assumption that the group that assembles for a private study period will be a heterogeneous group. Does this imply that the role of the teacher in charge must be purely supervisory? Surely not! **Young students can benefit greatly from the interest and involvement of a teacher who is not acting in his/her role of subject specialist.** Many teachers underestimate their own general expertise in such matters as use of language, analysis of meaning, strategies for solving problems, strategies of acquiring information, study skills, and so on.

This suggests a much more active role for the private study supervisor, and a more suitable title should be used: *Learning Support Tutor? Private Study Coordinator?* Here are some of the likely tasks for such a role:

- Setting up a system of individual action plans *(see above)*.
- Arranging *ad hoc* groupings of students for mutual aid.
- Acting as a sounding board to hear plans of work and strategies for solving problems.
- Coaching individuals or small groups in subject areas where the teacher feels fairly confident.
- Encouraging students to be active in pursuit of their own learning needs, especially in the wider use of resources (including people).

At first students need the scope and the limitations of the arrangement explained to them. They are so used to dealing with teachers only in their role as subject specialists. But when they have become accustomed to the system they will value the support received as a legitimate contribution to their learning progress which is complementary to the support they get from their subject specialists.

Use of technology

There is now a wide range of technological support available to the teacher and it is rapidly increasing. The benefits are seen as follows:

☐ Vast amounts of information can be stored and made instantly accessible to the learner who can analyse and transform it in a variety of ways.

☐ Records can be kept of student performance, interests, or needs.

☐ Guidance can be offered according to the total information that is available to the system.

☐ Specific teaching tasks can be undertaken, using a carefully designed structure and sequencing, and also operating interactively with the learner.

☐ Control of experiments and simulations can have the effect of extending the experience and the environment of the learner.

The implications are that the teacher's role as main provider of information is diminishing and a new role as **manager of the learning process** is on the increase. Here are some of the components of that new role from the point of view of technology.

☐ All teachers need a good understanding of the range of technological capabilities and some experience as a user of them.

☐ The school needs to consider how learners get access to technology. They may need frequent and instant access - so centralisation of equipment may be the wrong decision.

☐ Teachers need to plan their students' use of technology as an exercise in the management of individual and small group work. This means that individual work plans and small group tutoring are the techniques which will help the teacher to manage the work more effectively.

Technology, far from removing the need for a teacher, actually makes more demands on the teacher's organising skills.

7

Flexible Forms of
Assessment

Profiling

Records of Achievement

Continuous Assessment

Credit Transfer

The Effects of the National

Curriculum

FLEXIBLE FORMS OF ASSESSMENT

There is a clear trend in assessment which matches the movement towards greater flexibility in teaching and learning. The trend is made up of the following emphases:

☐ **A desire to extend the range of achievements and experiences which are recorded about a student.**

For the school as a whole this means everything about the student which is relevant to his/her personal, social and academic development. For the individual teacher or department it means extending the record well beyond the simple mastery of knowledge which used to be the sole record, and enhancing the record so that it provides a clearer and fuller picture of what the student knows, understands, and can do.

☐ A desire to involve the student as much as possible in the process of making decisions about assessment and in the keeping of the records.

☐ A desire to make the process of assessment continuous so that it can be a formative influence as well as providing a summative report.

☐ A desire to cast assessment and the processes of teaching and learning in the same mould, so that the philosophy and styles are consistent within the total educational experience.

A ## Profiling

Profiling is the continuous assessment that is made as part of the normal activity of the classroom. It aims to broaden the base of the assessment and to involve the student. This is the tradition of the best practice in the profession, and there has been considerable high quality development work in recent years. It is a tradition which is being followed by the National Curriculum; the *Standard Assessment Tasks (SATs)* (at least for younger students) are to take the form of extended classroom activities - part of the teaching and learning process.

Facing all the changes there is a need for teachers to develop their skills in designing (or adopting) and operating good systems of profiling. For the teaching within a given subject these seem to be the desirable elements of such a system:

1) Determine what capabilities you want to develop in your students - what it is that they should know, understand or be able to do.

2) Organise these decisions into a meaningful structure (headings and sub-headings).

3) Describe, as far as possible, exactly what these desirable capabilities will look like.

4) Devise a simple system for recording the assessments. A two-dimensional grid serves well.

5) Make appropriate arrangements for negotiation and decision making involving teacher and student.

6) Make arrangements for the keeping of the record. It is most desirable that the student should have responsibility for keeping at least a copy of the record. If this is organised in a folder, many other items of value and significance can be included.

The most important point about profiling is that it can only be accomplished successfully where teaching and learning are organised on flexible lines.

There is much to be said for making profiling decisions **during group tutorials**. In this way it really does become thoroughly integrated with the teaching and learning programme. It is much more economical of the teacher's own time, and there is also the benefit of the mutual support and interest throughout the group.

B   Records of achievement

A record of achievement is the natural result of assessment by profiling. While the accumulation of the detail of the record may have taken place over a period of time, the record is usually regarded as a summary of achievements and experiences at the end of a course of study. It aims to be a comprehensive statement which will not only give satisfaction to the student but will also be of practical use to employers and other educational institutions.

Profiling and records of achievement are part of the same process, and the principles which have been described for profiling apply equally to both. **Records of achievement and flexible learning are inter-dependent.** Records of achievement can only flourish where flexible learning methods are being used, and it is impossible to envisage successful flexible learning without a comprehensive record of achievement as an important outcome.

The record of achievement is truly comprehensive. Typically it might consist of the following:

- Personal qualities
- A personal record of interests, activities and achievements
- A summary of courses followed
- Assessments of performance in specific subjects of the curriculum
- Assessment of skills which are cross-curricular (examples are oracy, literacy, numeracy, I.T. skills, study skills, communication skills, and problem solving)
- Examination certificates
- Examples of work, particularly those which have been done independently and over a period of time.

The sheer size of the task is daunting, especially if it is regarded as an additional load for which additional time has to be found. It is far better to regard it as an integral part of the normal teaching and learning process and to assimilate it. This inevitably points to the **group tutorial** as the main vehicle for delivering records of achievement.

We have already described the group tutorial conducted by the subject specialist and also the group tutorial conducted by the general tutor who has an overall responsibility for the guidance and support of the learner. If these two are used the assimilation of records of achievement seems possible. Both parties need to be clear as to who will record what information and how it can best be coordinated from the two tutorials.

C Continuous assessment

The introduction of the Standard Grade and then GCSE encouraged many teachers to look at the possibilities of more flexible ways of organising teaching and learning. These Examinations emphasise (a) coursework and continuous assessment, and (b) practical, problem solving approaches, oral work, and communication skills.

Coursework and continuous assessment puts greater demands on the students, and there has been much anxiety about the load of work and responsibility carried by many students. Those who choose a number of subjects with heavy project work demands, can find that the burden is extreme. They are required to perform in long range planning, organisation, careful sequencing of tasks, trial and error, and formative evaluation at every stage. This is asking too much of the average 15 and 16 year old. So the management problems for the teacher who needs to support all this are formidable.

It is probably fair to claim that the full aims of GCSE and Standard Grade will not be adequately met until teachers achieve competence in the management and conduct of small group tutorials.

D   Credit Transfer

Credit transfer is the arrangement whereby a student is able to transfer a credit gained within one examination system into another system. The arrangement works best where the course structure is modular. This means that a student can deal in quite small parts of an educational programme and treat them as separate entities for the purpose of accumulating credits leading towards an award. Credit transfer makes a valuable contribution towards flexibility. It means that a student can avoid falling through the gaps in the system and can adapt sensibly to changing needs and situations.

The greatest need for credit transfer is beyond the age of 16 where the number of possible courses and qualifications proliferates. There has been much effort in recent years to provide a more coherent framework which will give an assurance of progression and transferability.

Recent proposals give cause for much hope. The request that curriculum and qualifications bodies should get together on core skills across the academic/vocational divide is a welcome initiative. This means opening up a range of non-GCE courses to A-level students. For example, short courses approved by the National Council for Vocational Qualifications include credits in *information technology, modern languages*, and *communications skills*. The availability of such modules should help to raise the appeal of post-16 education.

E   The Effects of the National Curriculum

It is much too early gauge the likely effect of the National Curriculum. The assessment arrangements are to be an important part of the whole initiative. The question which is still unanswered is to what extent the proposed testing will impose more rigid procedures on classroom work.

The indications given so far for the testing of seven year-olds are that the standard assessment tasks will take the form of extended classroom activities based around the kind of topics which teachers themselves would set up. **So assessment should become part of the teaching and learning process.**

How far will this philosophy and style will extend up the range? It is much too early to say !

8

Systems of
Flexible Learning

Resource-based Learning

Supported Self-Study

Open Access Workshops

Open Learning (Institution based)

Distance Learning

Definitions and Categories

SYSTEMS OF FLEXIBLE LEARNING

There have been many systems of organising teaching and learning
which are based on a broad student-centred philosophy both in this
country and abroad. This small selection of initiatives is confined to the
UK and to the last two decades.

A

Resource-based learning

This term was first used by a Nuffield Foundation project set up in the
late 60's to examine the possibilities of a shift towards more
student-centred styles in the secondary schools. The first effects of the
initiative were in two broad directions:

1) A number of schools, encouraged by a Schools Council project,
   concentrated their efforts on the school library. The library
   became multimedia and resources production was often
   associated with it. Teachers began devising resource-based
   learning projects which involved heavy use of a wide range of
   resources. Many libraries were renamed 'resource centres'.

2) Many schools concentrated their efforts on resource-based learning
   within the classroom. Teachers often worked extremely hard to
   devise worksheets which would encourage students to work *at their
   own pace*.

The Nuffield work was continued by a joint project of the DES and
Avon County. The brief for this project was to help schools produce the
right kinds of learning materials for student-centred learning. However
this project identified an even greater need namely the need for
experiment and training in the management of student-centred learning.
It was argued that the student on independent learning programmes has
a greater need of the teacher, not less. The term **'classroom
management'** was used to emphasise the complexity of the tasks facing
the teacher who aspired to organise student-centred learning.

B

Supported self-study

This term was introduced by the National Council for Educational
Technology in 1981. The original idea was to use a form of
independent learning to help schools overcome the problems of very
small uneconomic groups which would be the result of falling rolls.

However, it soon became apparent that the schools' interest was in
student-centred learning in its own right, not as a weapon for solving

administrative problems, although a small number of schools certainly did find it possible to maintain some minority subjects with reduced contact time and a supported self-study approach.

The main thrust of the NCET project was to emphasise the importance of the tutorial support of the independent learner - hence **supported** self-study. This is particularly interesting because educational technologists first came to independent learning through their work on programmed learning in the 60's. This was based on a 'behaviourist' psychology - clear statements of objectives, together with stimulus/response processes of learning. But the way that supported self-study has developed within the secondary schools owes much more to the 'humanistic' school of thought with its emphasis on helping the student to discover the personal meaning of new information and ideas.

C   Open access workshops

These workshops have been a common feature in colleges of FE and some sixth form colleges. The idea is to provide in a centre a range of self-study materials which students can access on a 'drop in' basis. So students can follow whole courses this way or use the centre for special needs - remedial work, support courses, and so on. The arrangements for tutoring vary considerably. All institutions claim that there tutorial support is available, but it is not common for tutorial support to be a built-in requirement. Much tutorial support is, in fact, on demand.

D   Open Learning (institution based)

Open learning has been offered at a large number of colleges of FE. The main characteristics of these programmes have been as follows:

- ☐   A strong reliance on specially prepared open learning 'packages' which aim to provide all, or nearly all, the student's resource needs.

- ☐   An educational technology approach to learning, particularly in vocational subjects where the skills to be taught can be accurately described and easily tested.

- ☐   Tutoring support which tends to be nearer to general counselling and advice than to the close academic support that is offered in supported self-study. This, of course, is a generalisation. The actual arrangements do vary considerably from very close support at the one extreme to a very loose advisory service if the student wants it.

E

Distance learning

There is very little pure distance learning in the schools. In further education however some students do find it necessary to register for courses through a correspondence system. This particularly applies if a student lives a long way from a centre or if the course is so specialised as to be offered by only one centre in the country. Distance learning is not desirable or necessary for the majority of school students most of the time. But where a school is interested in preparing its students for life-long learning it may be no bad thing to give students the experience of learning at a distance at least on one small module during the latter years of a school career.

F

Definitions and Categories

Some writers have expended much time and energy on definitions and categorisations. It seems that there is a proliferation of terms in use and confusion must surely result. There is however another way of looking at this.

It could be argued that it is wrong to try to define different systems or methods in teaching and learning. Instead it might be more valuable to concentrate simply on **good teaching and learning** and to give some idea of its desirable attributes. This will emphasise much more that **variety** is a key virtue in teaching and learning and that adopting a particular 'system' can have the effect of narrowing the range of teacher capabilities and student experience. Here are some suggestions as to the attributes of good teaching and learning:

- ☐ **A variety of styles and techniques are regularly used.** This would therefore include inspiring whole-class teaching, as well as well-organised small group and individual work.

- ☐ **Arrangements** which create the environment for teaching and learning are **flexible** with the needs of the student constantly at the fore.

- ☐ The **resources** which provide the data and stimuli for learning should be drawn from as **wide a range** of sources as possible.

- ☐ The **teacher** should create frequent opportunities to work **personally** with students in very small groups in order that his/her example and influence should be maximised.

- ☐ In every way the work within classes should be **student-centred**, and flexibility should be used in order to achieve this.

If this approach is adopted there is no longer any need for the different terms, and teachers will be free of this feeling of *'yet another initiative'*. The purpose of this handbook was to describe what is meant by flexible learning. In effect, it concludes by saying it doesn't matter. What **does** matter is what happens in the classroom or wherever teachers and students meet.

What they call it is of less importance than what they actually do. **They should just call it good teaching and learning.**

Appendix 1

The Flexible Learning Project

This national project started in April 1989, initially for a one year period, but has now been extended to 1993. It is supported by the Training Agency as part of the extension of TVEI. It aims to promote flexible learning - a broad concept which embraces most of the student-centred approaches which are being developed in the schools.

The project works mainly through a network of regional project leaders who have been appointed by consortia of local authorities. The responsibilities of the regional project leaders are:

- information
- consultancy
- training
- networking.

In addition a number of small projects work nationwide to provide guidance and support to the whole Project in special ways. Examples of this work are:

- Developments of supported self-study materials.
- Case studies of whole school approaches to flexible learning.
- Developments of flexible learning approaches in sixth form mathematics.
- Developments of training materials for teachers.
- Developments in inter-active video.
- Review of current materials available to support flexible learning approaches.
- Development of database and information services.
- Studies of the implications for LEAs.

Details of the national projects can be obtained from:

TVEI, B5,
St Mary's House,
Moorfoot,
Sheffield
S1 4PQ.

Regional Project leaders can be contacted at the following addresses:

Scotland   **Marion Docherty/Peter Gilmartin**
                                      TVEI Centre
                                      Flemington Road
                                      Glenrothes
                                      Fife
                                      K97 5QS

Wales   **Wynne Jones**
                                      West Glamorgan Enterprise Trust
                                      11 St Mary's Square
                                      Swansea
                                      SA1 3LD

North East   **Angela Nichols**
                                      Flexible Learning Centre
                                      South Tyneside College
                                      Mill Lane
                                      Hebburn
                                      NE31 2ER

Yorkshire and Humberside   **Mel Rockett**
                                      Flexible Learning Project
                                      Park Grove School
                                      Dudley Street
                                      York
                                      YO3 7LG

North West   **Margaret Waring/Judy Gilmour/Terry Richmond**
                                      Flexible Learning Project
                                      North Cheshire College
                                      Padgate
                                      Warrington
                                      WA2 9OB

East Midlands   **Jim Houghton**
                                      The Centre for Educational Technology
                                      Herrick Road
                                      Leicester
                                      LE2 6OJ

South East   **John Webb**
                                      Flexible Learning Centre
                                      Sandown Court School
                                      Blackhurst Lane
                                      Tunbridge Wells
                                      TN2 4PY

West Midlands	**Jeff Morgan/ John Bethel/ Steven Bending** Flexible Learning Project Portway Educational Development Centre Laburnum Rd Kingswinford DY6 8EH
Eastern	**Avrille Close** Education Department Shire Hall Castle Hill Cambridge CB3 0AP
North Thames	**Michael Betts/ Chris Haines// Julia Holland/ David Ware** Flexible Learning Project The Mansion Minchenden High St Southgate London N14 6BJ
Southern	**Brian Sutton** Portsmouth Teachers Resources Centre Sundridge Close Cosham Portsmouth PO6 3JL
South West	**John Brown** County Curriculum Centre Churchdown Lane Hucclecote Gloucester GL3 3QN

Appendix 2

Other Organisations supporting Flexible Learning

BBC Education Information
Villers House
The Broadway
Ealing
London
W5 2PA

Careers and Occupational
Information Centre
Training Agency
Moorfoot
Sheffield
S1 4PQ

Careers and Research Advisory
Centre
Sheraton House
Castle Park
Cambridge
CB3 0AX

Further Education Unit
Information Centre
2 Orange Street
London
WC2H 7WE

Open College
St James Building
Oxford Street
Manchester
M1 8DR

Open School
Foxhole
Dartington
Devon
TQ9 6EB

Open University
Walton Hall
Milton Keynes
MK7 6AA

National Council for Educational
Technology
Sir William Lyons Road
Science Park
University of Warwick
Coventry
CV4 7EZ

National Extension College
18 Brooklands Avenue
Cambridge
CB2 2HN

National Institute for Careers
Information and Counselling
Hatfield Polytechnic
Balls Park
Maugrove Road
Hertford
SG13 8QF

National Interactive Video Centre
32-34 Stephenson Way
London
NW1 2HD

NERIS
Maryland College
Leighton Street
Woburn
Milton Keynes
MK17 9JD

Wolsey Hall
66 Banbury Road
Oxford
OX2 6PR

The Local Authorities

This is perhaps the best source of help and guidance since many local authorities now have an adviser or advisory teacher working within the broad field of flexible learning.

Unfortunately there are many different job titles and this can be confusing. But usually people with titles which include any of the following expressions are likely to be closely in touch with developments in flexible learning:

- resource-based learning
- open learning
- active learning
- supported self-study
- teaching and learning styles.

Appendix 3

Selected List of References

This very small selection has been made with these questions in mind:

1) Does the book offer practical guidance to teachers charged with the task of organising flexible learning?

2) Does it deal with a fair number of the key issues in flexible learning?

3) Does it serve as a gateway to other sources of reference?

Each of the books below seem to satisfy at least two of the above tests.

Department of Education and Science (1988). Secondary Schools: An Appraisal by HMI. HMSO.

Hopson B and Scally M (1980). Lifeskills Teaching. McGraw Hill.

Lewis R ((1986). The Schools Guide to Open Learning. National Extension College.

Lincoln P ((1987). The Learning School. British Library.

Marland M ((1981). Information Skills in the Secondary Curriculum. Methuen Educational.

Miller J C ((1982). Tutoring: the Guidance and Counselling Role of the Tutor in Vocational Preparation. FEU.

National Extension College/ National Council for Educational Technology (1989). Implementing Flexible Learning: A Resource Pack for Trainers.

Oldroyd, Smith and Lee. School-based Staff Development Activities. Longmans Resources Unit.

Rainbow R (1987). Making Supported Self-Study Work. NCET.

Taylor L C (1972). Resources for Learning. Penguin.

Thomas J B ((1980). The Self in Education. NFER.

Waterhouse P (1983). Managing the Learning Process. McGraw Hill.

Waterhouse P ((1988). Supported Self-Study: An Introduction for Teachers. NCET.

Index

The Teaching and Learning Series

This book, *Flexible Learning, An outline,* is the first in the series and is followed by others which examine in more depth some of the issues raised.

Book 2, *Classroom Management,* by **Philip Waterhouse,** provides a detailed insight into the management of a wide variety of teaching and learning strategies. It provides practical advice on:

- Planning and organisation of schemes of work
- Differentiation
- Assignments
- Management of resources
- The organisation and layout of classrooms
- Assessment and recording
- Managing the whole class, small group and individual work.

The book will be a valuable handbook for both classroom teachers and for those managing teaching and learning in schools and colleges.

ISBN 1 85539 004 3   £4.50   To be published Summer 1990

Book 3, *Resources for Flexible Learning* by **Robert Powell,** provides practical advice on the complex question of resources.

- Defining flexible resources
- Choosing and evaluating resources
- Adapting existing resources
- Making full use of libraries/resources centres
- Creating and writing original resources
- Preparing study guides
- Planning and writing assignments
- Thinking about design and layout
- Using desktop publishing.

The book will suggest ways in which teachers and students can use a wide variety of resources both to satisfy the demands of the national curriculum and to develop independent learning skills.

ISBN 1 835539 005 1   £4.50   To be published Summer 1990

Book 4, *Tutoring,* by **Philip Waterhouse** explores the possibilities of skilful tutoring. It presents clearly:

- The rationale and objectives of tutoring
- The contexts for tutoring
- Arrangements for tutoring
- Tutoring styles
- Tutoring techniques

The book will serve as an invaluable handbook for all those seeking to provide guidance and support to students both in the classroom and in more informal learning situations.

ISBN 1 85539 006 X   £4.50   To be published Summer 1990.

Book 5, *What makes a good school?* by **Tim Brighouse** identifies those features of school organisation and management which are essential elements of successful teaching and learning. It examines:

- Leadership in the successful school
- Environment in the successful school
- Staff development in the successful school
- Collective review in the successful school
- School and curriculum development planning
- The organisation of learning in the successful school
- Successful teaching and learning

ISBN 1 85539 007 8   £4.50   To be published Autumn 1990.

This book is an introduction to a major series by **Tim Brighouse** (Research Machines Professor of Education, University of Keele) which explores each of the topics in some depth. This series will be published by Network Educational Press in 1991.

All books in the Teaching and Learning series £4.50, discounts available for bulk orders direct from the publishers. Order forms and further details from:

Network Educational Press, PO Box 635, Rode, Bath, BA3 3FB.

Tel: 0373 830833

Other titles from Network Educational Press

Coursework Enquiry/Study Guides

introduced by **Philip Waterhouse**

A series of photocopiable coursework enquiry/study guides is available in the following subject areas:

- □ Geography
- □ Humanities
- □ Business Studies
- □ English Literature (available September 1990)

Each subject pack contains 30 different enquiries on a wide range of topics. The guides provide:

- clear practical guidance
- advice on resources, activities and presentation
- scope for the individual group or class investigations
- flexibility in use.

50,000 of these guides have been purchased by schools and colleges since their publication in May 1989. They have been purchased for use in:

- Geography, Humanities and Business Studies (13-16)
- English (13-16)
- General Studies (14-18)
- Personal and Social Education (14-18)
- CPVE (16+) and BTEC. (16+)

They have been ordered by those with cross-curricular interests such as:

- TVEI Co-ordinators
- Flexible Learning Co-ordinators
- Librarians and resource centre managers
- Open Learning Co-ordinators
- Teacher and resource centre wardens.

Each pack £35.00. A full set of Geography, Humanities and Business Studies £95.00. Brochures and order forms from the publishers.

Network House, PO Box 635, Rode, Bath, BA3 3FB. Tel: 0373 830833

Marketing Open Learning
by Direct Mail

by Ian Hunter and David Beeson

Open Learning is booming - it is the ideal answer for a growing number of people and organisations:

- For businesses seeking to enhance the skills of their workforce.
- For individuals retraining in response to technological and social change.
- For members of the public making use of increased leisure time.

Open Learning is attractive because it is:

- flexible
- cost-effective
- responsive to individual need.

Educational establishments facing falling roles, reduced income and staff redundancy, can take advantage of this boom. But they cannot expect business to *walk through the door* - potential clients need to be aware of the opportunities that exist. **Open Learning, like any other product, needs to be marketed.**

The authors, from the world of Open Learning and commercial Marketing, argue that **direct mail** is the most effective marketing strategy. The book provides a step-by-step guide:

- Why Marketing?
- Identifying and creating the demand
- Targeting potential clients
- Creating a mailshot
- Making use of computers
- Evaluating the competition
- Organising the campaign.

The book is essential reading for both College Managers and Open Learning Coordinators and will provide invaluable advice in the promotion and sale of Open Learning opportunities to the local community.

ISBN 1 85539 009 4   Available direct from the publishers Network Educational Press at £12.50. To be published May 1990.